Monopolies and the People

by Charles Whiting Baker

TO ALL THOSE WHO LOVE TRUTH AND JUSTICE AND EQUITY, WHO VALUE OUR HERITAGE OF LIBERTY AND PEACEFUL FRATERNITY, AND WHO ARE WILLING TO UNITE IN UPHOLDING AND DEFENDING THE COMMONWEALTH--THAT PRESERVER AND PROTECTOR OF THE RIGHTS OF THE WHOLE PEOPLE--THE AUTHOR DEDICATES THIS WORK.

PREFACE.

In the following pages it has been my endeavor to present, first, the results of a careful and impartial investigation into the present and prospective status of the monopolies in every industry; and, second, to discuss in all fairness the questions in regard to these monopolies--their cause, growth, future prospects, evils, and remedies--which every thinking man is to-day asking.

The first part of this task, the presentation of facts with regard to existing monopolies, may seem to the well informed reader to be imperfectly done, because of the host of powerful and important monopolies of every sort that are not so much as mentioned. But I have deemed it most important that the broad facts concerning monopolies should be widely known; and I have, therefore, aimed to present these facts in a readable and concise way, although, in so doing, only a few of the important monopolies in each industry could be even mentioned. It is to be hoped that no one will underrate the importance of the problem of monopoly, or question the conclusions which I have reached, because of these omissions. To any such readers who may not be satisfied from the facts hereafter given that monopolies are the salient feature of our present industrial situation, and, moreover, that they have come to stay, I would recommend a careful perusal of the financial and trade journals for a few months.

Wherever possible I have presented actual statistics bearing on the question at issue; but as regards trusts, monopolies in trade, mining, labor, and in fact nearly all monopolies, there are no statistics to be had. Nor can any be obtained, for it would be absurd for the government to collect statistics of the operation of that which it pronounces illegal but makes no effort to punish.

It may increase the respect of some readers for the conclusions I have reached, to know that it was a practical acquaintance with monopolies rather than any study of economic theories which led me to undertake the present work; that, at the time I undertook it, I was wholly undecided as to the proper remedies for monopolies, and was quite willing to believe, if the facts had proved it to me, that they were destined to work their own cure; and that the rapid growth and increase of monopolies in very many industries, in the few months since these chapters were written, have furnished fresh evidence that my conclusions have not been amiss.

Finally, I wish to place all emphasis on the fact that all the great movements toward genuine reform must go hand in hand. The cause of the people is one cause, and those who work for honest officers in our government, pure elections, the suppression of crime and pauperism, the mental and moral elevation of men and women, are striking harder blows at monopolies than they may realize. But if they desire to hasten the day of their success, they must bring the great masses of the people to comprehend that these movements aim at nothing less than their complete deliverance; and that the reformers who labor so earnestly to make our government purer and its people nobler, heartily desire also to cure the evils of monopoly, and to serve the cause of the people in its every form.

CHARLES WHITING BAKER.

TRIBUNE BUILDING, New York City. June, 1889.

MONOPOLIES AND THE PEOPLE

I.

THE PROBLEM PRESENTED.

The word "trust," standing for one of the noblest faculties of the heart, has always held an honorable place in our language. It is one of the strange occurrences by which languages become indelible records of great facts in the history of the world, that this word has recently acquired a new meaning, which, to the popular ear at least, is as hateful as the old meaning is pleasant and gratifying.

Some future generation may yet be interested in searching out the fact that back in the nineteenth century the word "trust" was used to signify an obnoxious combination to restrict competition among those engaged in the same business; and that it was so called because the various members of the combination entrusted the control of their projects and business to some of their number selected as trustees. We of the present day, however, are vitally interested in a question far more important to us than the examination of a curiosity of philology. We are all of us directly affected to-day by the operation of trusts; in some cases so that we feel the effect and rebel under it; in other cases, so that we are unconscious of their influence and pay little heed to their working.

It is but a few months since public attention was directed to the subject of trusts; but, thanks to the widespread educational influence of the political campaign, at the present day the great proportion of the voters of the country have at least heard of the existence of trusts, and have probably some idea of their working and their effect upon the public at large. They have been pointed out as a great and growing evil; and few speakers or writers have ventured to defend them farther than to claim that their evil effects were exaggerated, and predict their early disappearance through natural causes; but while remedy after remedy has been suggested for the evil so generally acknowledged, none seems to have met with widespread and hearty approval, and practically the only effect thus far of the popular agitation has been to warn the trust makers and trust owners that the public is awakening to the results of their work and is likely to call them to account.

The truth is, as we shall see later, that it is a difficult matter to apply an effective remedy of any sort to the trusts by legislation, without running counter to many established precedents of law and custom, and without serious interference with what are generally regarded as inalienable rights. Yet we are making the attempt. Already legislative and congressional committees have made their tours of investigation, and bills have been introduced in the legislatures of many of the States, and in Congress, looking to the restriction or abolition of trust monopolies.

It is the wise surgeon, however, who, before he takes the knife to cut out a troublesome growth, carefully diagnoses its origin and cause, determines whether it is purely local, or whether it springs from the general state of the whole body, and whether it is the herald of an organic disease or merely the result of repressed energies or wrongly-trained organs. So we, in our treatment of the body politic, will do well to examine most carefully the actual nature of the diseases which we seek to cure, and discern, if we can, the causes which have brought them on and tend to perpetuate them. If we can discover these, we shall, perhaps, be able to cure permanently by removing the ultimate cause. At any rate, our remedies will be apt to reach the disease far more effectually than if they were sought out in a haphazard way.

The crudest thinker, at the first attempt to increase his knowledge of the general nature of trusts, discovers that the problem has a close connection with others which have long puzzled workers for the public good. Trusts ally themselves at once in his mind with monopolies, in whichever form he is most familiar with them, and are apt to be classed at once, without further consideration, as simply a new device for the oppression of the laborer by the capitalist. But the man of judicious and candid mind is not content with any such conclusion; he finds at once, indeed, that a trust is a combination to suppress competition among producers of manufactured goods, and he calls to mind the fact that other combinations to suppress competition exist in various other lines of industry. Surely when the governing motives are so similar, the proper remedies, if remedies are needed, cannot be greatly unlike. And though, taking the country as a whole, trusts have occupied more attention lately than any other form of monopoly, the problem of railroad monopoly is still all-absorbing in the West; in every city there is clamor against the burdens of taxation levied by gas, electric-light, street-railway, and kindred monopolies; while strikes in every industry testify to the strength of those who would shut out competition from the labor market. These and similar social and industrial problems are quite as important as the problem of trusts, and their solution is becoming every day more urgent and necessary. If we neglect them too long, or carelessly adopt some unsuitable or unjust remedy, who knows the price we may pay for our folly in blood and treasure?

The problem before us, then, as we see it from our present standpoint, is the problem of monopoly. What is it? Whence comes it? What are its effects? And, most important of all, what ought we to do about it? Surely questions whose correct answer is of such importance to the welfare of each person and to the very existence of society demand the careful consideration of every thinking man.

Let us then take up this problem and give it the fairest and most candid investigation possible. In order to do this, let us remember that the truth is the object of our search, and that it will be necessary, if the conclusions from our investigation are to be of value, that we divest ourselves, so far as possible, of all preconceived opinions founded, perhaps unconsciously, on the statements or evidence of incompetent authorities, and also of all prejudices. Let us, in searching for facts and principles, examine with impartiality the evidence and arguments which each side presents, and judge with candor between them.

The author wishes to make an earnest personal request to the reader who is minded to follow the discussion through the following pages, that he will in good faith attempt to do this thing: that he will lay aside for the present his opinions already formed, as the author himself has conscientiously aimed to do while pursuing this investigation, and give a fair hearing to both sides of the question. A complicated machine can only be understood when it is viewed from different standpoints. So, here, in order to find the truth, we must examine trusts from the standpoint of the trust maker as well as from that of the consumer; and trade unions, from the standpoint of their members as well as from the ground of employers and of the public at large. We shall indeed meet much error by this method of study, but is it not proverbial that there are two sides to every question? It will be our task to study these opposing views and sift from them the truths for which we seek.

In taking up now the problem before us, let us adopt the true scientific method for its solution. We must first find out as fully as possible the actual facts with regard to monopolies of every sort and the competition which monopoly replaces. Next, by discussing and comparing the evidence obtained, we may be able to discover the natural laws by which competition and monopoly are controlled; and finally, with our knowledge of these, we will try to discover both the source of the evils which vex us and the proper methods for ameliorating, curing, or preventing them, whichever may be found possible.

Such is the outline of the investigation before us, which it may as well be said here could easily be extended and amplified to fill many volumes. The author has preferred to prepare the present volume without such amplification, believing that the busy men of affairs, to whom a practical knowledge of the subjects herein treated is most essential, have, as a rule, no leisure for the extended study which the volumes into which the present one might easily be expanded would require. He trusts, however, that brevity will not be found wholly incompatible with thoroughness; and that the fact that much which might have properly been included in the book is omitted, will not be taken as a necessary indication that the conclusions arrived at are without value.

II.

TRUSTS AND MONOPOLIES IN MANUFACTURING INDUSTRIES.

In common use the word "trust" is at present rather loosely used to denote any combination formed for the purpose of restricting or killing competition. Properly speaking, however, a trust is a combination to restrain competition among producers, formed by placing the various producing properties (mills, factories, etc.) in the hands of a board of trustees, who are empowered to direct the operations of production and sale, as if the properties were all under a single ownership and management.

The novel characteristic of the trust is not the fact that it is a monopoly, but that it is a monopoly formed by combining several competitors according to a new plan. The process of placing property in the hands of trustees is familiar to every business man. In the formation of a trust the different firms or companies who have been competing with each other in the production and sale of goods agree to place the management of all their several properties in the hands of a board of trustees. The powers of this board and its relation to the owners of the various properties are ingeniously devised to evade the common law, which declares that contracts in restraint of competition are against public policy, and illegal.

The first of the modern trusts was the Standard Oil Trust, which was a combination formed among several of the refiners of crude petroleum in the States of Pennsylvania and Ohio in the year 1869. The original combination grew out of the control of certain important patents connected with the process of refining. It pursued its course for a number of years without attracting much attention outside of the centre of its operations; but of late years so much has been published in regard to it that the very word "Standard" has come to be almost a synonym for monopoly. It is probable that certain branches of the iron and steel trade were the next to be combined by means of a trust, but as these were arrangements between private firms, not much information as to the time of their origin has reached the public. The second great trust to attract general public attention was the American Cotton Oil Trust, in which some of the same men who have so successfully engineered the Standard Oil combination are heavily interested. These two great trusts, the Cotton Oil and the Standard, have attracted widespread attention, and, to a certain extent, the public has become familiar with their organization and plan of operation; but popular feeling on the subject was not fully aroused until 1887, when the newspapers of the country made generally known the fact that the trust principle of combination was being rapidly adopted by the manufacturers of a large number of important lines of goods. The effect which these monopolies were believed to have upon the public welfare was pointed out by writers and speakers, and Congress and the State Legislatures were besought to investigate these combinations and seek to suppress them. Meanwhile it seems to be true that the popular agitation has had no effect in lessening the number of trusts, or checking their formation and growth; and they continue to increase and to gather their profits, while the public impotently wonders what it is going to do about it. Let us be careful, however, to make no assumption that the trust is injurious to the public at large. That is a matter which is before us for investigation.

It is safe to assume that the reader is somewhat familiar with the general charges which have been brought against the trusts; but even if this side of the story has not been heard, it is not unfair to look at them first from the standpoint of the men who make and manage them. In order to do this, suppose we select some particular trust which will serve as a type, and imagine that some frank, candid manufacturer, who is a member of this trust, comes before us to give an account of its formation and operations. This man comes, we suppose, not as an unwilling informant, or as one on trial. He is frank, honest, and plain-spoken. He talks as man to man, and gives us, not the specious argument of an eloquent pleader in defence of trusts, but just that view of his trust and its work that his own conscience impels him to take. Certainly, then, he deserves an impartial hearing.

A number of years ago the principal manufacturers of linseed oil in the United States formed an association. It was started largely for social ends, and was very successful. Business men are generally most interested in their own plans and operations; and those who are familiar with the same topics and have similar interests and purposes are apt to make agreeable companions for each other. We discussed many points connected with the management of our business at the meetings, and by interchanging with each other our views and experiences with different devices, methods of management, etc., we were able to get much valuable information, as well as social pleasure, from meeting one another.

Now within the past few years things have been going from bad to worse with the manufacturers of linseed oil. The long and short of it all was that the margin between the cost of the raw seed and running our mills, and what we could get for the oil cake and the linseed oil in the market, has grown exceedingly narrow. It's hard to tell just what has caused it. They say over-production; but what has caused the over-production? One thing that may have had something to do with it is the new mills they have been putting up in the Northwest. Many of the Eastern mills used to get large quantities of seed from Iowa; but they are building cities out there now, as well as raising flax-seed, and when they were booming some of those cities they would raise heavy bonuses in aid of new enterprises. Among these were some great linseed oil mills, which have loaded up the market pretty heavily of late years; so that not only has the price sagged down, but we have all had to work to get rid of our stocks. The firms which had the best mills and machinery, and were in a position to get their seed reasonably and put their goods on the market with least expense for transportation, etc., have been making a small profit over and above their expenses. But some of the works which had to bring their seed a long way, and which haven't quite as good machinery as can be had now, were in a bad way. There were some of the oldest houses in the trade among them, too, and with fine men at their head. It was too bad to have them go under. They tried to cut down expenses, but strikes and trouble with their men prevented their saving much in that way. Then there was one item of expense which they had to increase instead of cutting down: that was the cost of marketing. Competition was so fierce, that, in order to keep up their trade, they had to spend more on salaries of expensive salesmen, and in advertising and pushing their goods, than they would dream of ordinarily.

It seemed too bad to cut each other's throats in that way, for that was what it amounted to, and when the association met,--or what was left of it, for the business rivalries had grown so bitter that many of the former personal friendships between the members had become strained and one after the other had dropped out,--the situation was discussed by the few members who met together. It was discussed earnestly, too, by men who felt an interest in what they said, because unless some remedy could be devised, they had got to sit still and watch the savings of a lifetime slip through their fingers. One thing was very clear to all. Though competition was as sharp as any one could possibly wish, the public was not getting such a wonderful benefit after all. Prices were not so very much lower for oil, nor higher for seed. It was the selling expense which had run up to a ruinous figure; and on one point all the members were unanimous,--that if all the firms in the trade could only work together in harmony in marketing their goods, they could save enough in salesmen's salaries, etc., to make a great difference in the profit-and-loss account without affecting the selling prices in the market one penny.

Another very important matter, which we had to handle pretty tenderly in our discussions, was that of adulteration. I must confess that a good many firms in the trade, who used to be above any thing of the sort, have been marketing some goods in the past few years which were not exactly the "pure linseed oil" which they were labelled. It's a mean business--adulteration,--but not many of our customers ever test their purchases. The one thing they are apt to look at is price, for they are buying to sell again; and when rivals are selling a cheaper oil that seems just as good until it is laid on as the pure linseed that you are obliged to ask a higher price for, the temptation to meet them at their own game, rather than lose your old customers, is a very strong one. Certainly, when competition took this form, it hurt the public even more than it hurt us. When people wish to buy pure linseed oil they ought to have some prospect of getting it, instead of getting an adulterated mixture of various substances; but at the rate competition was running, there seemed to be small prospect that there would be any really pure linseed oil put on the market in a short time. We have often discussed the possibility of stopping these adulterations, but it was a hard matter to cure by mere mutual agreement. How do I know what my competitor in a city a hundred miles away, does with the vats in his cellar after working hours, even if he has solemnly agreed not to adulterate his goods? For I must confess that there are a few men in our trade who are as tricky as horse jockeys.

Quite a number of improvements have been patented in linseed oil machinery in the past twenty years. Nothing wonderful, but things that effect little economies in the manufacture. We could have done without them; but when a few firms took them up, of course the rest had to follow suit, or fall behind in the race of competition. We have had to pay a heavy royalty on some of these machines, and it has been rather galling to count out our hard-earned dollars to the company which has bought up most of the patents, and is making 100 per cent. a year on what it paid for them, with no risk, and without doing a stroke of work. Now if we manufacturers could work in harmony, we could make this company come down from their high horse, and they would have to ask a reasonable price for their machines. But we could do more than this. It stands to reason that a good many improvements will be made in our machinery in the future. We don't object to paying a fair price to any inventor who will work out these new ideas for us; but it does seem unjust for him to go and sell them to some outside company for a song, and have that company bleed the users of the improvement for every ounce they will stand. Now, by working together, we can refuse to pay royalties on any thing new which comes up; but require, instead, that any new patent in our line be submitted to a committee, who will examine and test it; and if they find it to be of value, will purchase it for the use of all members of the association.

Some of the members thought this was as far as we ought to go. They were opposed to "trusts" on principle. But the great majority saw so clearly where we could continue to better ourselves that they became enthusiastic over it.

Some speculators, in years of short crops, have occasionally tried to "corner" flax-seed in a small way. We could refuse to buy except directly from the growers, and that branch of speculation would be a thing of the past. We have sent out some pretty sharp men as buyers, and sometimes they have bought flax-seed in some of the backwoods districts at very low rates. At other times, two buyers from rival firms have run counter to each other, and paid prices larger than their employers could really afford. But with our combination, we cannot only fix uniform prices for seed, but we can send out only enough buyers to cover the territory; and the work of buying is reduced to simply inspecting and weighing the seed.

Now another thing: Of course, not every manufacturer in the business owns his mills. It is a fact that since the close times of the past few years the majority of the firms are carrying mortgages on their mills; and some of them in the West are paying as high as eight or ten per cent. interest. But with the combined capital of all the firms in the trade at our back, we can change all that. Either by a guaranty, or by assuming the obligations, we can bring the interest charges on every mill in the association down to four or five per cent. at most.

We have been paying enormous rates to fire insurance companies. They are not as familiar with our business as we are ourselves, and they don't know just how much risk there really is; so they charge us a rate which they make sure is high enough. We can combine together and insure ourselves on the mutual plan; and by stipulating that each firm shall establish and keep up such precautions against fire as an expert may direct, we can not only reduce the cost of our insurance to that of our actual losses, but we can make these a very small amount.

It may be said that we might have done all these things without forming any trust to control prices. But the practical fact was that we could not. There was so much "bad blood" between some of the different firms in the business, from the rivalry and the sharp competition for trade, that as long as that was kept up it was impossible to get them to have any thing to do with each other in a business way. It was no small task to get these old feuds patched up; but some of the best and squarest men in the business went right into the work, and at meetings of the association, and privately, exerted all their influence to forward this coming together for mutual aid and protection. They did it conscientiously, too, I think, believing that it was necessary to save many of us from financial ruin; and that we were not bound, under any circumstances, to sacrifice ourselves for the sake of the public. The trust has been formed, as every one knows, and many of the things we planned to do have been already accomplished. We have stopped adulterations on all goods made by members of the trust; and the improvement in the quality of linseed oil which has been effected is an important benefit to the public. We are managing all the works in the trust as if it were all a single property, controlled by different managers; and the saving in expense, over the old plan of cut-throat competition, when everybody was striving to save himself and sink his rivals, is an enormous one.

One thing which has caused much hue and cry, is the fact that we have closed half a dozen mills or so. But the matter stood in this way: these mills were not favorably situated for doing business, all things considered; and all the mills in the country cannot run all the time, because there are more mills in existence than are needed to supply the market. These mills must have been closed soon, if the trust had not commenced operations, because they could not be run under the old regime and pay expenses. We knew we could make the oil at a less cost in our other mills, so we concluded to buy out the owners of these at a fair price, and shut up the works. Prices of linseed oil have been raised somewhat, we confess; but we claim that they had been forced down much too low, by the excessive competition which has prevailed for a few years past. Of course some of the most hot-headed and grasping among us, were anxious to force prices away up, when they once realized that we had an absolute monopoly of the linseed oil trade of the country; but the great majority were practically unanimous in a demand for just prices only, and the adoption of the policy of live and let live; for trust-makers are not entirely selfish.

We claim, moreover, that we are breaking no legal or moral law by this action. We are, for the most part, private parties or firms--but few corporations,--hence the attempt to abolish trusts on the ground that the corporations composing trusts have exceeded the power given by their charters will fail to reach our case. We have certainly done this: we have killed competition in the linseed oil trade; but we submit that with so many other interests and trades organized to protect themselves from outside competition, and control the prices at which their products are sold to the public, we were, in self-defence and for our own preservation, obliged to take this step.[1]

[1] It should be explained that the above is not given as a bona-fide statement of facts concerning this especial trust, but as a vivid description of the organization and plans of a typical trust, from the standpoint of its owners and managers.

Probably, too, few or no existing trusts have tried to benefit themselves in so many different ways as we have supposed this imaginary trust to have done. But to shorten our investigation, the author has purposely extended the scope of this trust's action, to bring out clearly the variety and importance of the methods by which a trust reaps profits, aside from any advance in the price of its product.

If we omit the references to the especial trade, the above view of a trust from the trust-makers' standpoint will do for almost any of the many combinations which have been formed by different manufacturers for the purpose of controlling production and prices. One thing is clearly indicated in the above, and will certainly be conceded: That the men who have formed these trusts are animated by the same motives as those that govern humanity in general. They have, in some cases at least, known what it was to be crowded close to the wall by severe competition. They all at once saw a way opening by which they could be freed from the worries and losses which had been making their business one of small and uncertain profits, and would be set squarely on their feet with a sure prospect for large and steady gains. It is using a common expression to say that they would have been more than human if they had refused to improve this opportunity. Certainly, then, in examining further the trusts, we shall do so with no feeling of personal prejudice toward the men who originated them and carry them on.

As we have given a hearing to the case from the trust-makers' standpoint, it is only fair that we should hear at equal length from the public who oppose the trusts; but to abbreviate the investigation, let us suppose that we are already familiar with the various charges which are brought against the trust monopolies, and let us proceed at once to consider the actual effect of the trusts upon the public.

Since we have heard so much in defence of the linseed oil trust, it will be well for us to inquire concerning the results, in which the public is interested, which have followed its organization. During the year 1887 (the trust was formed in January of that year) the price per gallon of linseed oil rose from thirty-eight cents to fifty-two cents; and this price was kept up or exceeded during 1888. That is to say, every purchaser of linseed oil, or every one who had occasion to have painting done, pays to the members of this trust, for every gallon of oil that he uses, about fourteen cents over and above the sum which he would pay if competition were allowed to do its usual work in keeping down prices.

What profits are the members of this trust making? Let us suppose that they were just able, at the old price of thirty-eight cents per gallon, to pay all their running expenses and four per cent. on the capital invested, making nothing for profits beyond a fair salary to the managers of the business. Then the gain of fifteen cents a gallon in the selling price is clear profit to them. Now add to this the fact, which was plainly brought out in the foregoing supposed statement by a member of the trust, that it is possible by means of the trust to greatly reduce expenses in many directions as well as to increase receipts, and we begin to form some conception of the profits which this trust is harvesting. If we wish to put the statement in figures, suppose we take the annual consumption of linseed oil in the country at thirty million gallons. Then the profits of the trust from the increased prices alone will amount to four and one half million dollars per annum.

There is another way in which trusts directly affect the public, which has received very much less attention than it deserves. Besides the people who use the linseed oil and pay the trust an extra fourteen cents a gallon for the privilege, there are a great number of people who would have used oil if the price had not advanced, but who cannot afford to do so at the advanced price. It is a well-known fact that every increase in the price of any article decreases the demand, and the advance in the price of linseed oil has undoubtedly had a great effect in decreasing the consumption of oil. So while it is undoubtedly true that at the trust's prices there are more linseed-oil mills in the country than are needed to supply its wants, yet if the prices were lowered to the point which free competition would fix, there would probably be demand enough to keep all the mills running. To the trust, then, must be ascribed the final responsibility for the stoppage of the mills and the loss of employment by the workmen. Nor does the effect upon the labor market stop there. From the fact that less people can afford to paint their houses, because of the higher price of the oil, it is certain that there will be less employment for painters; and as less paint is used, all those interested in and employed in the paint trade are sufferers. It is to be remembered that we are speaking of the linseed oil trust only to make the case more vivid. The principle is general and applies equally well to other trusts, as for instance to the loss of employment by thousands of men working in refineries controlled by the sugar trust, in the fall of 1888. Still another effect of this trust's action is to be especially noted: the fact that the diminished production of oil lessens the demand for seed; and also that in the purchase of seed, as well as in the sale of oil, the trust has killed competition. The trust may, if it chooses, fix uniform prices for the seed which it purchases; and the farmer can take the prices they offer or keep his seed. Fortunately the farmer can raise other products instead of flax-seed, and will do so if the price is lowered by any large amount.

One other possible mode of profit for the trusts, which, however, they are hardly likely to engage in--from their fear of public opinion, if for no other reason--lies in the power which they possess over the labor market. It will probably be conceded at once that the rate of wages in any occupation depends, among other things, upon the competition of the various workmen who seek employment in that occupation, and also upon the competition among those who wish to hire men to work at that occupation. It is plain that when the competition among employers to secure men is active, wages will rise; and when this competition falls off, wages will fall. Now the trust is more than a combination for selling purposes only. It is a combination of all the properties concerned under practically a single ownership. Clearly, then, as the various mills belonging to a single owner will not compete with each other in the employment of labor, the mills belonging to a trust will be no more likely to do so. Thus if it were not for the fact that the workmen are able to take up some other employment if their wages are too low, they would be absolutely obliged to take what wages, great or small, the trust chose to give, and would be as dependent for their food and clothing upon the trust as was the slave upon his master.

The question is often asked why trusts have not been formed before, and what the causes are which have started them up so rapidly in such varied lines of industry. There is certainly room for much honest difference of opinion in reference to these causes; but one cause concerning whose influence there can be no dispute is the culmination of the change from the ancient system of manufacturing to the modern. Let us briefly trace the manner in which this branch of civilization has grown: In the most primitive state of existence, each man procures and prepares for himself the few things which he requires. With the first increase in intelligence those of most skill in making weapons and preparing skins make more than they require for themselves, which they exchange with others for the products of the chase. The next step is to teach to others the special skill required, and to employ them to aid the chief workman. Conditions analogous to these existed down to the end of the last century. The great bulk of all manufacturing was done in small shops, each employing only a few workmen; and the manufacturer or master workman labored at the side of his journeymen and apprentices. The products of these little workshops were sold in the country immediately adjacent. Of course the number of these scattered shops was so great that the possibility of uniting all the manufacturers in any one trade into a single organization to prevent competition among them, was beyond the thoughts of the most visionary.

The present century has seen three great economic wonders accomplished: the invention of labor-saving machinery, greatly multiplying the efficiency of labor in every art and trade; the application of steam power to the propulsion of that machinery; and the extension over all civilized lands of a network of railway lines, furnishing a rapid, safe, and miraculously cheap means of transportation to every part of the civilized world. In order to realize the greatest benefit from these devices, it has become necessary to concentrate our manufacturing operations in enormous factories; to collect under one roof a thousand workmen, increase their efficiency tenfold by the use of modern machinery, and distribute the products of their labor to the markets of the civilized world. The agency which has acted to bring about this result is competition. The large workshops were able to make goods so much cheaper than the small workshops that the latter disappeared. Then one by one the large workshops were built up into factories, or were shut up because the factories could make goods at less cost. So the growth has gone on, and each advance in carrying on production on a larger scale has resulted in lessening the cost of the finished goods. Competition, too, which at first was merely an unseen force among the scattered workshops, is now a fierce rivalry; each great firm strives for the lion's share of the market. Under these conditions it is quite natural that attempts should be made to check the reduction of profits by some form of agreement to limit competition. Many plans have been tried which attempted to effect this by mere agreements and contracts, methods which left each property to the control of its special owners; but none have been permanently successful. By the trust plan of combination, the properties are practically consolidated; and the failure of the combination through withdrawal of its members is avoided. It offers to manufacturers, close crowded by competition, a means of swelling their profits and ensuring against loss; and encouraged by the phenomenal success of the Standard Oil combination, they have not been slow to accept it.

The point to which we need to pay especial attention, in the foregoing consideration of the causes which have produced trusts, is the fact that the cost of production is continually being cheapened as it is carried on a larger and larger scale. And because the cheaper mode of production must always displace the mode which is more expensive: as Prof. Richard Ely expresses it, "Production on the largest possible scale will be the only practical mode of production in the near future." We need not stop to prove the statement that the cost of production by the modern factory system is a small fraction of that by the old workshop system. The fact that the former has beaten the latter in the race of competition would prove it, if it were not evident to the most careless observer. But it is also a fact that the trust, apart from its character as a monopoly, is actually a means of cheapening production over the system by independent factories, for it carries it on a larger scale than it has ever before been conducted. Our review of the trust from the trust makers' standpoint showed this most forcibly; and we shall see more of it as we study further the methods by which the monopoly gains an advantage over the independent producer in dispensing with what we may call the waste of competition. In the argument presented by the Standard Oil Trust before the House Committee on Manufactures in the summer of 1888, occurs the following statement of the work which that monopoly has done in cheapening production:

"The Standard Oil Trust offers to prove by various witnesses, including Messrs. Flagler and Rockefeller, that the disastrous condition of the refining business and the numerous failures of refiners prior to 1875 arose from imperfect methods of refining, want of co-operation among refiners, the prevalence of speculative methods in the purchase and sale of both crude and refined petroleum, sudden and great reductions in prices of crude, and excessive rates of freight; that these disasters led to co-operation and association among the refiners, and that such association and co-operation, resulting eventually in the Standard Oil Trust, has enabled the refiners so co-operating to reduce the price of petroleum products and thus benefit the public to a very marked degree and that this has been accomplished:

"1. By cheapening transportation, both local and to the seaboard, through perfecting and extending the pipe-line system, by constructing and supplying cars with which oil can be shipped in bulk at less cost than in packages, and the cost of packages also be saved; by building tanks for the storage of oil in bulk; by purchasing and perfecting terminal facilities for receiving, handling, and reshipping oils; by purchasing or building steam tugs and lighters for seaboard or river service, and by building wharves, docks, and warehouses for home and foreign shipments.

"2. That by uniting the knowledge, experience, and skill, and by building manufactories on a more perfect and extensive scale, with approved machinery and appliances, they have been enabled to and do manufacture a better quality of illuminating oil at less cost, the actual cost of manufacturing having been thereby reduced about 66 per cent.

"3. That by the same methods, the cost of manufacture in barrels, tin cans, and wooden cases has been reduced from 50 to 60 per cent.

"4. That as a result of these savings in cost, the price of refined oils has been reduced since co-operation began, about 9 cents per gallon, after making allowance for reduction in the price of crude oil, amounting to a saving to the public of about $100,000,000 per annum."

Certainly it would seem that this is a strong defence of the trust's character as a public benefactor; but it is well to note that while it has been making these expenditures and reducing the price of oil to the consumer, it has also been making some money for itself. The profits of this trust in 1887, according to the report of the committee appointed to investigate the subject of trusts by the New York Legislature, were $20,000,000. The nominal capital of the trust is but $90,000,000, a large portion of which is confessedly water. In answer to the statement that the price of oil has been reduced steadily by the operations of the trust, it is charged that no thanks is due to the trust for this benefit. The trust has always wished to put up the price, but the continual increase in the production of the oil fields has obliged the trust to make low prices in order to dispose of its stock. There are also about one hundred independent refineries competing with the trust, and their competition may have had some influence in keeping prices down. It is undoubtedly true that the economy in the storage, transportation, and distribution of oil by the systematic methods of the Standard Oil Trust has made it possible to deliver oil to the consumer at a small fraction of its cost a decade ago. But it is also true that a good part of the reduction in the price of oil is due to the abundant production of the petroleum wells, which have furnished us so lavish a supply. The principal charges against this trust, made by those who were conversant with its operations, have never been that it was particularly oppressive to consumers of oil; but that, in the attempt to crush out its competitors, it has not hesitated to use, in ways fair and foul, its enormous strength and influence to ruin those who dared to compete with it.

In a later chapter we shall be able to study these more intricate questions regarding trusts with a better understanding of our problem. Let us pay some attention now to the growth of the trusts and of combinations in general for the purpose of limiting competition among manufacturers, which has taken place within the past few years.

According to the little book entitled "Trusts," by Mr. Wm. W. Cook, the production of the following articles was, in February, 1888, more or less completely in the hands of trusts: petroleum, cotton-seed oil and cake, sugar, oatmeal, pearl barley, coal, straw-board, castor oil, linseed oil, lard, school slates, oil cloth, gas, whiskey, rubber, steel, steel rails, steel and iron beams, nails, wrought-iron pipe, iron nuts, stoves, lead, copper, envelopes, paper bags, paving pitch, cordage, coke, reaping and binding and mowing machines, threshing machines, ploughs, and glass--a long and somewhat jumbled list, to which, however, at the present time, there should probably be added: white lead, jute bagging, lumber, shingles, friction matches, beef, felt, lead pencils, cartridges and cartridge-shells, watches and watch cases, clothes-wringers, carpets, coffins and undertakers' supplies, dental tools, lager beer, wall paper, sandstone, marble, milk, salt, patent leather, flour, and bread. It should be said that, as regards most of these combinations, the public is ignorant beyond its knowledge that some form of combination for the purpose of restricting competition has been formed. For the purpose of our present investigation it makes little difference just what this combination may be.

The salient facts for us to note are, that among the manufacturers of this country there has arisen a widespread movement to partially or wholly avoid competition in the production and sale of their goods; that in a very great number of manufacturing industries these combinations have progressed so far that their managers have been able to advance prices and check production; that some of these combinations have taken the form of trusts, and by this means have every prospect of maintaining their stability and reaping their enormous profits with the same permanency and safety as has their predecessor, the Standard Oil Trust; and, finally, that with this prospect before them, our manufacturers, as a class, would lose their reputation as shrewd business men if they did not follow out the path marked out for them, and combine every manufacturing industry in which combination is possible upon the plan of the trust.

In conclusion, it may be well to examine the statement attributed to Mr. Andrew Carnegie, that, "there is no possibility of maintaining a trust. If successful for a time, and undue profits accrue, competition is courted which must be bought out; and this leads to fresh competition, and so on until the bubble bursts. I have never known an attempt to defeat the law of competition to be permanently successful. The public may regard trusts or combinations with serene confidence."

Surely if this statement is true, we have little need for further examination of this subject. We have now knowledge enough of our subject to enable us to determine its truth or falsity. We have found in the actual trusts that we have examined none which have shown signs of succumbing to outside competition. More than this, however, we have seen that it is possible for a trust to carry on business and deliver goods to the consumer at much less cost than an independent manufacturer can. And as surely as this law holds that production on the largest scale is the cheapest production, so surely will the trust triumph over the independent manufacturer wherever they come into competition. If the trust were always content when its competitors were disposed of, to make only the profits which it could secure by selling at such prices as the independent manufacturers could afford, there would be less outcry against it. But with the consumers wholly dependent upon it for supplies, the prices are in the trust's hands; and the tendency is to reap not only the profits due to its lessened cost of production, but also all it can secure by raising the selling price without arousing too much the enmity of the public.

Clearly the trust is at once a benefit and a curse. Can we by any means secure the benefit which it gives of reduction in cost without placing ourselves at the mercy of a monopoly? This is the question which must occur to every thoughtful man. Before we can answer it, however, we must examine the effects of competition and monopoly in other industries.

III.

MONOPOLIES OF MINERAL WEALTH.

It is a well known historical fact that the extraction of metals and minerals from the earth has been more subject to monopoly than almost any other business. It was, and in a large part of the civilized world still is, esteemed a prerogative of the sovereign. Agricultural products have always been gathered from a wide area; manufactures were formerly the product of mean and scattered workshops; but in the working of a rich mine, there was a constant income more princely than was to be obtained from any other single source. Again, with all due respect to the traditions of former generations, it seems to have been thought that any thing to which no one else had a valid title belonged to the crown; and as no one was able to assert any stronger claim to the ownership of mineral wealth than that they had stumbled upon it, it was natural for the sovereign to claim it as his. We see thus the recognition at an early date of the inherent difference between natural wealth and that created by labor.

But coming down to the present time, it is evident that the business of extracting some of the rarer metals from the earth is peculiarly liable to become a monopoly. It is one of the new laws of trade, whose force and importance we are just finding out, that the ease of restricting competition varies with the number of competing units which must be combined. Our most valuable metal, iron, is so widely distributed that any attempt to control the whole available supply could not long be successful. But it is one of the peculiarities of modern industry that by its specialization it furnishes constant opportunities for the establishment of new forms of monopoly, whose power is not generally understood. In the manufacture of Bessemer steel, which has now largely displaced wrought iron in the arts, it is necessary to use an iron ore of peculiar chemical composition. This ore is found most abundantly and of best quality in the mines of the Vermilion range, lying about one hundred miles north of Duluth, Minn., and in the mines of the Marquette Gogebic, and Menominee regions in the north Michigan peninsula. According to good authorities, a combination more or less effective has been formed among the owners of all these mines; and the highest price is charged for the ore which can be obtained without driving the customer to more distant markets for his supply. Among the mines of this district, competition, if not entirely stopped, is greatly checked, and is likely soon to be entirely a thing of the past. It is an interesting fact that among the members of the syndicate which owns the principal mines in the Vermilion regions are some of the trustees of the Standard Oil Trust. It is stated that some of these mines have paid 90 per cent. per annum on their capital stock, which, it is to be noted, represents a much greater sum than the amount invested in the plant of the mine.

It is thus apparent that the mining of the raw ore from which iron is made, abundant and scattered though it is, is not free from monopoly. The combinations to restrict competition among the makers of cast iron and of steel belong properly under the head of monopolies in manufactures. We need only refer here to the fact that they are supposed to exist and have more or less control of the market.

Fortunately for the stability of our system of currency and of finance, the precious metals, through the small ratio which their current production bears to the world's stock, and the fact that this stock is scattered among an enormous number of holders, are safe from any attempts to establish a monopoly to control their price through the control of their production. Other metals, however, which are like silver and gold in being found in workable deposits at but a few points on the globe but are there found in abundance, are peculiarly adapted to facilitate the schemes of monopolists. Of lead, copper, zinc, and tin, we require a steady supply for use in the various arts; and the statement has been made that the supply of each one of these is in the hands of a trust. To see the effect which these combinations have had on prices, let us examine the prices which have prevailed for two years past on these four articles, as shown in the following table:

Table of wholesale prices (cents per lb.) in New York City of copper, lead, tin, and zinc during 1886, 1887, and 1888:

	Copper	Lead	Tin	Zinc
1885 Dec. 31	11.50	4.60	-	5.35
1886 Apr. 3	11.45	4.90	-	5.50
1886 July 3	10.00	4.90	-	5.60
1886 Oct. 7	11.00	4.35	-	5.60
1887 Jan. 5	12.25	4.75	24.50	6.42
1887 Apr. 6	11.00	4.75	24.50	6.50
1887 July 6	10.50	4.92	25.00	7.00
1887 Oct. 6	11.00	4.45	23.30	6.75
1887 Dec. 29	17.75	5.00	37.00	6.00
1888 Mar. 29	17.50	5.50	39.50	6.75
1888 July 3	17.25	4.25	22.00	6.50
1888 Oct. 4	18.50	5.75	26.00	6.75
1889 Jan. 3	17.50	3.85	22.00	5.50
1889 Apr. 29	16.50	4.25	23.00	6.50

Taking the evidence of this table, we conclude that the combination which is said to control the zinc and lead markets is probably not a trust, but a "Producer's syndicate" or corner. The prices of lead show no such firm tendency to advance as would be expected if the production was in the hands of a single combination.

The prices of zinc, however, show a decided advance in the past two years over the prices for the three years preceding, the average price for 1886 being but 5.50, while for 1887-8 it is 6.58. This is a rise of no small importance, and the way it is maintained seems to give evidence of restriction of competition among producers.

But the striking fact in the above table is the evidence it presents of the work which has been done by that most gigantic and daring combination for the suppression of competition ever organized, the French Copper Syndicate or La Society Industrielle Commerciale des Metaux. This syndicate of French capitalists began operations in 1887, with the intention of "cornering" the tin supply of the world. The rise in price which was due to their operations is shown in the above table. But before completing their scheme they relinquished it for a grander enterprise, which would embrace the copper production of the world. They made contracts with the copper-mining companies in every country of the globe, by which they agreed to purchase all the copper which should be produced by the mines for three years to come at the fixed price of 13 cents per pound, and a bonus of half the profit which the syndicate was able to make from its sales to consumers. In effect this move killed the competition in the copper trade of the world, and placed every consumer at the mercy of this Paris syndicate. The advance in tin was of short duration, and those who suffered by it were speculators rather than consumers; but the advance in copper, as shown by our table, is still firmly maintained, and its effect on the industries using copper has been seriously felt all through 1888. In October, 1888, the Society extended its contracts with several mining companies to cover a period of twelve years, and advanced its price to the producers to 13?cents per pounds. At the same time, to avoid the accumulation of stock, which the diminished consumption consequent upon the increased price had caused, and which it had been generally predicted would finally be the cause of the Societies downfall, they arranged for the restriction of the production of the mines. If the Society which is backed by the heaviest capital, and managed by the shrewdest business skill of France, does what it intends to do, and its tributary producers are faithful to their contracts, for ten years to come, yes, for all years to come--for it is not likely that an enterprise of such golden returns will ever be abandoned if it can once profitably be carried out,-- the world must pay for its copper whatever these monopolists demand.

Probably the argument against the private ownership and control of the wealth which nature has stored up for the whole world's use was never brought home to men's minds so forcibly as it has been by the acts of these French speculators. Copper is a necessity to the industries of civilized society; and the mind of every unprejudiced person protests against the injustice of placing in the hands of any single firm or combination the power to exact such prices as they choose for the great staples of human consumption. This increase of price of about 7 cents per pound is a tax which affects, directly or indirectly, every person in the civilized world. Let us inquire what becomes of this tax. Perhaps 2 cents per pound will go into the pockets of the Frenchmen who have engineered the combination, a sum which will give them, if we set the annual consumption of copper at 400,000,000 pounds, a comfortable net income of about $8,000,000 per annum. The lion's share of the profits is taken by the producers, however; who, if 10 cents is the price at which copper would sell if free competition were in force, are receiving under the present contract with the Society about 5 cents per pound as a reward for their co-operation in its monopolistic scheme.[2]

[2] Since the above was written the collapse of the copper syndicate has taken place. The causes which brought this about were the failure to complete the contracts for restriction of production, and lack of funds to meet the current liabilities. The reason for both these must be largely ascribed to the fact that it had come to be generally realized how great and how obnoxious the monopoly was; and capitalists rightly feared that government interference would be interposed to check the monopoly's operations. If the syndicate had made its long-time contracts at the start, or if it had been bold and shrewd enough to have inveigled speculators on the bear side of the market into operating against it, M. Secretan and his associates might have won as many millions as they could have wished. It is a significant fact that the downfall of the syndicate was not followed by the reestablishment of free competition. Instead there was at once talk of another syndicate being formed to hold the copper stored up by the Society and keep the price up as long as possible. On this side of the water the question was at once canvassed whether a combination could be formed among the different American companies to prevent competition and support the price. Evidently the failure of this scheme has not discouraged the makers of monopolies.

It is appropriate here, too, to make reference to the enormous profits which the owners of the copper mines of the country are receiving, apart from the special influence of this great syndicate. The richest and most valuable copper mines in the world lie on the southern shore of Lake Superior. The Calumet and Hecla Company, which works one of the richest deposits of native copper ever found, has a capital stock of $2,500,000, on which it has paid, since 1870, $30,000,000 in dividends. The reports of these companies to their stockholders show that the present cost of refined copper at the mines is as low as 4 cents per pound, and its cost, delivered in the New York market, is only 5?cents.

Probably the officers of these companies are right in their belief that in no other mines of the world can copper be produced so cheaply. But the question that comes with force to every thinking man is: If the wealth of the ore in these mines is so much greater than that in any other that it can be produced at so much less cost, does there not exist here a natural monopoly, of which the owners of these mines are getting the sole benefit? And, again, by what right does the chief benefit from this rich deposit accrue to the few men who own the mines, rather than to the many men in all parts of the world who wish to use their product?

Great and important as is the copper monopoly, of far greater importance to us than any and all the combinations in the metal industries are the monopolies which control the price of coal. We do not often realize how intimately connected is our nineteenth-century civilization with the store of fuel laid up for us in distant geologic ages. And in this country, with our severe climate, coal is all-important as a factor of domestic economy, as well as a necessity to manufacturing and metallurgical industries. The total cost to the consumers of the coal used in the United States every year (about 120,000,000 tons), calling the average retail price $4.00 per ton, is nearly $500,000,000, or over $8.00 per annum for every man, woman, and child in the country. Surely, then, the statement which we make at the outset, that the coal trade of the United States is in the hands of monopolists; and that competition, where not killed, is almost impotent to keep down prices, is one which merits earnest attention.

The United States possesses coal fields of enormous extent and richness. The mineral is widely distributed, too, productive mines being now in operation in 27 of the States and Territories. Anthracite coal, however, which is by far the best adapted to domestic use, only occurs in a limited area in the State of Pennsylvania; but here the deposit is of phenomenal richness. The total area of the Pennsylvania anthracite field is about 300,000 acres. Of this area nearly 200,000 acres is owned by seven railway corporations. These companies, either directly or through subsidiary companies controlled in the same interest, carry on mining operations, carry the coal to market, and sell it. The following figures[3] exhibit the receipts of each of these companies from sales of coal from their mines during the year 1887:

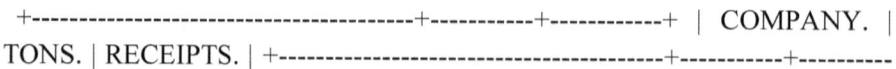

```
+------------------------------------------+-----------+------------+    |  COMPANY.  |
TONS. | RECEIPTS. | +-------------------------------------+-----------+----------
```

Philadelphia and Reading R. R. Co.	7,555,252	$18,856,550
Central R. R. Co. of N. J.	4,852,859	12,132,146
Lehigh Valley R. R. Co.	5,784,450	14,461,125
Del., Lackawanna, and Western R. R. Co.	6,220,793	19,044,803
Delaware and Hudson Canal Co.	4,048,340	10,100,118
Pennsylvania R. R. Co.	3,818,143	8,820,718
New York, Lake Erie, and Western R'y Co.	2,363,290	6,846,342
Total	34,643,127	$90,261,805

[3] Compiled from "The Coal Trade," 1888, (H. E. Saward), and "Poor's Manual of Railroads," and partially estimated.

Thus these seven corporations alone produced from their own mines, carried to market, and sold, over 34,000,000 tons of coal during the year, for which they received about $90,000,000. Of the magnitude of the operations carried on by these great corporations we now have some idea. Let us next inquire to what extent competition is allowed to act between them to keep down prices.

Many years ago these seven companies formed the famous anthracite-coal pool. This was an agreement by which all the companies concerned agreed to maintain a uniform selling price for coal at all important distributing points where two or more of the companies came into competition. Some of the prices which were fixed by the pool were extremely arbitrary. Cities in Pennsylvania within an hour's ride of the coal fields had to pay nearly as high a price for coal as those 500 miles or more distant. Rates of transportation on coal mined by individual operators were made such that the latter could not afford to sell below the prices fixed by the pool, even if they had been so disposed. At the present time the situation has been modified by the long and short-haul clause of the Interstate Commerce law, by which the railroad is obliged to make its transportation rates somewhat proportionate to distance, and also by the passage of a law in the State of Pennsylvania, by which the acts of the anthracite-coal pool were declared illegal and punishable. Nominally, therefore, the pool is a thing of the past; but the practical fact is, that by secret or tacit agreement the various companies are not competing with each other any more now than in the days of the pool, and at points like New York or Buffalo, where two or more roads meet, the same prices are quoted by each different company.

Nor are the charges against the pool comprehended in its autocratic determination of the price of coal. To make production correspond with price, it was necessary at times to close collieries entirely, throwing the miners out of employment. The individual operators, too, have no love for the combination. Their profit depends more than any thing else on the rate of transportation, and thus whether they shall make or lose depends on the railroad companies. They claim that the railways base their rates for carrying coal upon the principle of "charging what the traffic will bear." This is a matter, however, which we can better discuss in the next chapter.

It is thus evident beyond dispute that the production of anthracite coal in this country is an industry uncontrolled by competition. To sum up: these seven great corporations own more than two thirds of the area in which workable anthracite coal is found: they mine and market directly the great bulk of the total production; the individual operators are dependent on the railways for getting their coal to a market; and the price at which they can afford to sell it depends on the railroad rates. Finally, consider that these seven companies work in harmony, both as to traffic rates and prices for the sale of coal, and the conclusion is irresistible that competition in anthracite-coal production in the United States is practically dead.

Let it be noted, for the benefit of those who may conceive that the above statement is unfair to the railway companies, that no charge is here made that the prices fixed by the companies for the coal are at the present time extortionate or unjust. That is a separate matter; in which, doubtless, there would be plenty to affirm on the one hand that the prices charged were no more than a just compensation, while their opponents would declare that the prices adopted by the pool favor some points to the prejudice of others, and that the statement that they were on the whole exorbitant was proven by the fact that the railway lines in the coal regions, where honestly managed, have paid great dividends on the actual capital invested.

Compared with the production of Pennsylvania anthracite, the coal production of any other single section seems small. But it is only so by comparison, for the Western coals, while inferior in quality, are abundant and easily mined, and must remain the staple for general consumption throughout the region west of the Mississippi, as well as for large sections further east.

As is well known, the people of the Western and Northwestern plains are wholly dependent upon the railroads for their supplies of every description, except the raw products of the soil. The railways themselves are great consumers of coal, and have bought up large tracts of coal lands and opened mines. In the desire to develop traffic and ensure a supply of coal to the settlers on their lines--we will even say of cheap coal,--the railway companies have entered the coal trade themselves, either directly or through subsidiary companies. Thus it comes about that hundreds of thousands of people of the West and Northwest must pay for coal, which is an absolute necessity of life during several months of the year, whatever price the managers of a single railway corporation may demand. Let it be understood that no charges are here made of injustice or extortion on the part of the railway companies. It is only wished to bring out the fact that competition is here wholly absent. It is believed that, in some cases at least, an honest attempt has been made to mine and sell the coal at merely a fair profit. But in days to come it will not be so directly for the interest of the railways to deal liberally with their patrons as at present. Other men of less breadth and principle and more ready to grasp at a chance for enormous profits may control the company's affairs; and if that happens, the opportunity to take advantage of the absence of competition and raise the price of coal will be utilized.

A brief review of the actual status of the coal production of the West and South will help us to a clear appreciation of the case. The Missouri Pacific Railway Company, through subsidiary companies, extracted from its mines in Missouri and the Indian Territory, during 1887, 1,618,605 tons of coal. Through its control of transportation rates, private operators have been compelled to sell coal at the company's prices in the market. The company has recently purchased large tracts of coal lands in Colorado, on which it is opening mines. The Atchison, Topeka, and Santa F? the Chicago, Burlington, and Quincy, the Denver and New Orleans, the Union Pacific, and the Denver and Rio Grande Railway companies are also heavily interested in the Colorado coal mines. The last company has long held a bonanza in the monopoly of the coal mining and transportation for the Colorado silver-mining and smelting districts. Though the other companies, to which the Rock Island should probably be added, come in as competitors, there can be no doubt that their active competition will be of short duration. The Wyoming coal fields are being worked by the Union Pacific and the Chicago and Northwestern companies, while the Chicago, Burlington, and Quincy and a company supposed to be closely connected with the Northern Pacific are preparing to take the field at an early date. On the Pacific coast the coal trade has long been a monopoly in the hands of the Oregon Railway and Navigation Company, who have kept the prices in San Francisco just below the point at which it becomes profitable to import Australian coal. Other railways are now preparing to reach the coal fields, but can we doubt that the competition to which the coal consumers are looking with eager anticipation will prove evanescent? Returning to the East, we find the coal mines of northern Illinois all held by a single company, which has full control of the traffic; while the mines of southern Illinois, on which the St. Louis consumers depend, are united as the Consolidated Coal Company. This latter corporation has "wrecked" many of its mines for the purpose of limiting the supply and raising the price; and has bought many mines of competing companies and closed them for the same purpose. The Attorney-General of Illinois has been requested to bring suit against this "trust" for the forfeiture of its charter.

In the Hocking Valley coal fields in Ohio, the Columbus, Hocking Valley and Toledo Railway Company owns 10,000 acres of coal lands, and mined, in 1887, 1,870,416 tons of coal. The coal in western Virginia is coming into the hands of the Norfolk and Western Railroad Company, while the coal of Alabama, of which so much has been noised abroad, has been quietly gathered in by the Louisville and Nashville corporation. The Tennessee Coal and Iron Company, which owns 76,000 acres of coal lands, and mined 1,145,000 tons in 1882, is owned by parties largely interested in the East Tennessee, Virginia and Georgia Railroad system. West Virginia has probably the most valuable untouched coal deposits of any State in the Union, but these also are rapidly being gathered up by railway corporations.

To sum up, in the words of one of the best informed authorities, the coal business of the country is at the mercy of the railroads.

It is to be noted, however, that this is simply the result of natural causes. Railway managers, in seeking to develop and place on a sound basis the mineral properties which could furnish a heavy and profitable traffic to their lines, have only done what they regarded as their duty to the owners of their roads. And that this policy has effected a rapid development of our resources is beyond question.

The combinations to restrict competition among bituminous coal producers have been of a very different sort from those in force among the anthracite producers. The soft-coal fields are so widely scattered that it has never been possible to combine all the producers so as to control prices by a single authority. Local combinations, however, controlling all the fields of a single locality, have long been an important feature of the trade, and have been able to control prices pretty absolutely within their respective localities. The fact that the principal item in the cost of coal is transportation, enables a combination covering all the producers of a certain field to raise prices very notably before competitors can afford to ship from other coal-producing districts.

It would seem that our fuel is especially liable to be subjected to monopoly, for, as we have already seen in the preceding chapter, the control over the petroleum trade is held by the Standard Oil Trust. How much of the production of crude petroleum is in the hands of the trust it is hard to say. This much is certain, that there is a "Petroleum Producers' Association," which has a compact enough organization to be able to make contracts with the Standard Oil Company regarding the limitation of production. It is even stated that the Standard Oil Trust itself controls to a considerable extent the oil-producing territory; but this is hardly probable.

Our newest and most wonderful fuel, natural gas, has already come under the control of a few great corporations, who own the wells and the pipes for conveying and distributing it to the consumers. A striking instance of the arbitrary nature of prices when under a monopoly's control was shown at Pittsburgh a few months ago. As is well known, upon the introduction of natural gas to that city a great number of the manufactories, as well as the private houses, discarded coal, and at considerable expense fitted up boilers, furnaces, etc., to use the new fuel. After the use of the gas had become general and its value had come to be thoroughly understood, the company furnishing the supply advanced the rates 100 per cent., without previous notice; and despite the remonstrance of indignant consumers, the advanced rate had to be paid or the use of the gas discontinued, the latter alternative involving the loss of the money invested in piping, burners, etc.

Of the minor products of mines and quarries, marble, sandstone, borax, salt, and asphalt are all known to be more or less thoroughly under the control of monopolies, which, though less important and powerful, show the same tendency toward the destruction of competition.

Great as is the extent to which the monopoly of the mineral wealth of the world has gone, we can scarcely doubt that if the movement is unchecked it will go much farther. In one sense the only absolute necessaries of life are food and clothing. But to the civilization of to-day the metals and minerals are no less indispensable; and these cannot be made anywhere, like manufactured goods; or grown on wide areas, like the products of the soil. We are absolutely at the mercy of the men who own our deposits of coal and copper and lead, and it is only to be expected that they will take greater advantage of their legal industrial advantage. The combinations that exist will be made stronger and more binding, and new ones will be formed. The French copper "corner" has taught men that under the broad protection of International law their schemes of industrial conquest may embrace the world; and it is not to be doubted that the temporary "corner" will yet result in a strong permanent combination; and that the precedent set by this successful monopoly will be eagerly followed by those who wish to secure like profits by the control of some other form of mineral wealth.

IV.

MONOPOLIES OF TRANSPORTATION AND COMMUNICATION.

We have already alluded to the fact that the concentration of manufacturing in large mills at great commercial centres has been made possible by the development of railway transportation, and that the rapid settlement of our Western prairies is due to the same agency; but it is worth while to note more fully the difference between ancient and modern conditions in the business of transportation.

In the first place, it is plain that no more than a century ago the world had comparatively very little need for railways. Each community produced from its farms and shops most of the things which it needed; and the interchange of goods between different sections, while considerable in the aggregate, was as nothing in comparison with modern domestic commerce. The king's highways were open to every one, and though monopolies for coach lines were sometimes granted and toll roads were quite common, there was no possibility for any really harmful monopoly in transportation to arise, because the necessity of transportation was so small. Some writer has ascribed all the evils of modern railway monopolies to the fact that in their establishment the old principle of English common law that the king's highway is open to every man, was disregarded. But if we sift down this ancient maxim of law to its essential principle, we find it to be, there must be no monopoly in transportation; and the problem of obtaining the advantages of modern railway transportation and keeping up, at the same time, the free competition that exists in transportation on a highway is seen to be as far from solution as before.

The importance of our railway traffic is proven by statistics. Of the total wealth annually produced in this country, it is probably a fair estimate to say that ten per cent. is paid for transportation of the raw material and finished goods in their various journeys between producers, dealers, and consumers, and for transportation of passengers whose journeys directly or indirectly contribute to the nation's industry. That is to say, the gross yearly earnings of all the railroads and transportation lines of the country is about one tenth of the total value of all the year's products. The average is brought down by the amount of sustenance still consumed in the locality where it is produced, and by the amount of valuable merchandise. But of the bulky products like coal and grain, the greater part of the cost to the remote consumer is due to the cost of carriage.

It is also necessary to a proper appreciation of the problem, that we understand that railway transportation is now as absolutely necessary as is the production of food and clothing. Annihilate the railway communications of any of our great cities, and thousands would perish by starvation before they could scatter to agricultural regions. There was great suffering in many small communities in Minnesota and Dakota in the severe winter of 1887-8, because the heavy storms blockaded the railroads and prevented them from bringing in a supply of coal and provisions. But it is not taking the question in its broadest sense to consider whether we could eke out an existence without railway communication. The fact is that under modern conditions every man obtains all the things which he desires, not by producing them himself, but by producing some one thing which others desire. The interchange between each producer and each consumer must, broadly speaking, be all made by means of the railway; and without that, stores, factories, mills, mines, and farms, would have to cease operation.

Remembering now the importance and necessity of transportation, let us inquire how the price at which it is sold to the public, the rate of fare and freight, is fixed. Is it or can it be generally fixed by competition?

There are now in the United States about 37,000 railway stations where freight and passengers are received for transportation. Now, from the nature of the case, not more than ten per cent. of these are or can be at the junction of two or more lines of railway. (By actual count, on January 1, 1887, eight per cent. of existing stations were junction points.) Therefore the shippers and buyers of goods at nine-tenths of the shipping points of the country must always be dependent on the facilities and rates offered by a single railway. Such rates of transportation as are fixed, be they high or low, must be paid, if business is carried on at all. And when we consider the ten per cent. of railway stations which are, or may be, junction points, we find that at least three-fourths of them are merely the junction of two lines owned by the same company. Consolidation of railway lines has gone on very rapidly within the past few years and is undoubtedly destined to go much further. Of the 158,000 miles of railway in the country, about eighty per cent. is included in systems 500 miles or more in extent; and a dozen corporations control nearly half of the total mileage. The benefits which the public receive from this consolidation are so vast and so necessary that no one who is familiar with railway affairs would dream of making the suggestion that further consolidations be stopped or that past ones be undone.

There is a great tendency on the part of the public, however, to look with fear and disfavor on further railway consolidation. And because this is so, it is greatly to be desired that the beneficial effects of consolidation should be better understood. The most important benefits are included under one head, the saving in expense and the avoidance of waste, and this is effected in very many different ways. Suppose a great system like the Pennsylvania or the Chicago & Northwestern were cut up into fifty or sixty independent roads, each with its own complete staff of officers. Each road would have to pay its president, directors, and heads of operating departments, would have to maintain its own repair-shops, general offices, etc., and conduct in general all the business necessary to the profitable operation of a railway corporation. A car of wheat or a passenger in going from Chicago to New York would have to be transferred from one road to another at perhaps twenty different points, and the freight or fare paid would be divided among twenty different companies, with corresponding clerical labor. The modern conveniences of through tickets, through baggage-checks, and through freight shipments, would be difficult, if not impossible. Further, consolidation tends to produce vastly better service and greater safety. The large systems can and do employ the highest grade of talent to direct their work. Every thing is systematized and managed with a view to producing the best results in efficiency and safety with the least waste of material and labor. And while the improvement in safety and convenience is all for the benefit of the public, a large part of the saving in expense effected by consolidation has likewise come back to the patrons of the roads in the form of reduced rates of fare and freight.

It is difficult, however, for any one not familiar with the technical details of the railway business to fully appreciate the importance and necessity of the consolidations which have been effected, and the grave results that would follow the realization of the mad proposition to set us back a half century by cutting up our railroad systems into short local lines. It must be plain to every one, however, that while the loss of all the benefits of consolidation would be certain, the gain in competition could affect only the few junction points; and as we shall now see, the effect even on them would be small.

Assuming that the total number of railway junction points in the United States is 3,000, we find, on examination, that at about two-thirds only two lines meet, and at more than half the remainder only three lines meet. It is plain that in the vast majority of cases where two roads intersect, and in many cases where three or four come together, the lines meet perhaps at right angles and diverge to entirely different localities. The shipper bringing goods to the station, then, may choose whether he will send his goods north or east perhaps; but only in the few cases where two lines run to the same point does he really have the choice of two rates for getting his produce to market. Practically, then, there are not, and never can be, more than a few hundred places in the country where shippers will be able to choose different routes for sending their goods to market. We say there never can be, because the building of a line of railway to parallel an existing line able to carry all the traffic is an absolute loss to the world of the capital spent in its construction, and a constant drain after it is built in the cost of its operation. This fact is now, fortunately, generally appreciated.

But what of the competitive traffic which exists between commercial centres, like the trunk-line traffic between Chicago and the cities on the seaboard, or between the former city and the collecting centres farther west like St. Paul, Omaha, and Kansas City? Here, indeed, there is competition; and it is of great importance because of the enormous bulk of the traffic which traverses these few routes.

It is a peculiar feature of the railway business which we have now to consider, and one which is not generally understood. We have already perceived the principle that competition cannot permanently exceed a certain intensity; and the proof of this principle in the case of the railway is remarkably plain. Suppose two roads are competing for the traffic between Omaha and Chicago. A shipper at the former city who wishes to send a few tons of freight to Chicago may go to one company and ask their rates, then to the other and induce them to give him a lower rate, and then back to the first again, until he secures rates low enough to suit him. Now it is a fact that either company can afford to carry this especial freight for less than the actual cost of carrying it better than it can afford to lose the shipment. This is because it costs the company practically no more to carry the goods than if they were not shipped by its line; and hence whatever is received for the freight is so much profit. Stated in the form of a principle, this fact is expressed thus: Receipts from additional traffic are almost clear profit. Nor is this all. The practical impossibility of distinguishing additional traffic from other traffic, and the enactment of State and National laws requiring uniform rates to be charged, places all traffic on a common basis; and the same cause which makes it more profitable to carry additional traffic for a song than to lose it, makes it better for a railroad to carry traffic, temporarily at least, for less than the actual running expenses of the road, rather than to lose it. The train and station service, the general office and shop expenses, must all be kept up, though the freight and passengers carried dwindle to almost nothing; and the capital invested in the road is a total loss, unless the line is kept in operation and earns some income, even though it be small. This last influence, as we shall see later, is a most important and far-reaching one in its effect on industrial competition.

The cause of the intensity of competition in railway traffic is now evident. And from what we have seen, it follows that two railway lines competing freely with each other cannot possibly do business at a profit. Let us see what are the actual results of this law of practical railway management. Evidently the managers of two competing railway lines have but two possible courses open. They may, by tacit or formal agreement, unite in fixing common rates on both the roads, or they may attempt to do business with free competition. But we have already proven that the latter course must result in reducing the income of the road certainly below the amount necessary to pay the operating expenses and the interest on the bonds, and probably it will be insufficient to pay the running expenses alone. The inevitable result, then, is the bankruptcy of the weaker road, the appointment of a receiver, and its sale, in all probability to its stronger competitor. This is the chain of cause and effect which has wrought the consolidation of competing parallel roads in scores of cases, and which, if free competition is allowed to act, is sure to do so.

We can now appreciate the necessity which managers of competing lines are under to agree upon uniform rates for traffic over their roads, and at the same time the difficulty of doing this. The strange paradox is true that while it is necessary to the continued solvent existence of the competing corporations that such an agreement be made, it is also greatly to their advantage to break it secretly and secure additional traffic. It is necessary, therefore, that the parties to the agreement be strongly bound to maintain it inviolate; and to effect this, "pools" were established. In pooling traffic, each company paid either the whole or a percentage of their traffic receipts into a common fund, which was divided among the companies forming the pool, according to an agreed ratio. Under this method it is evident that all incentive to secret cutting of rates and dishonest methods for stealing additional traffic from another road was taken away.

How widespread and universal is the restraint of competition by railway corporations may be seen by the following pithy words, penned by Charles Francis Adams, President of the Union Pacific Railway:

"Irresponsive and secret combinations among railways always have existed, and, so long as the railroad system continues as it now is, they unquestionably always will exist. No law can make two corporations, any more than two individuals, actively undersell each other in any market, if they do not wish to do so. But they can only cease doing so by agreeing, in public or private, on a price below which neither will sell. If they cannot do this publicly, they will assuredly do it secretly. This is what, with alternations of conflict, the railroad companies have done in one way or another; and this is what they are now doing and must always continue to do, until complete change of conditions is brought about. Against this practice, the moment it begins to assume any character of responsibility or permanence, statutes innumerable have been aimed, and clauses strictly interdicting it have of late been incorporated into several State constitutions. The experience of the last few years, if it has proved nothing else, has conclusively demonstrated how utterly impotent and futile such enactments and provisions necessarily are."

Disregarding for the present the latter part of the above quotation, consider the statement that during the whole history of railway corporations, agreements to restrain competition have been the rule. This the slightest research proves to be an historical fact, and it is in perfect accord with our preceding statement, that such agreements were necessary to the solvent existence of railway corporations. The records also show that invariably when these agreements have been broken and competition has been allowed to have full play, the revenues of the roads have been rapidly reduced to a point where, unless a peace was effected, bankruptcy ensued.

Mr. Adams said, with truth, that no law had proven of any effect in preventing these competition-killing agreements between railways; but since the above extract was written, the Interstate Commerce law has been enacted. Let us pay some attention to its working and results. It is a curious fact that the framers of railway legislation in this country, almost down to the present time, have concentrated all their energies on the endeavor to keep up free competition; and the Interstate law is no exception to this rule. The plan of the Interstate law was about as follows: "Here are a few dozen great commercial centres where the railway lines of different systems meet. We will first prohibit the pooling by which they have restricted competition at these points. Then, in order that the thousands of other shipping points shall receive an equal benefit, we will enact a 'long and short haul clause,' obliging the rates charged to be in some degree proportionate to the distance. Thus competition at the great centres will bring rates down everywhere, and the public will be benefited."

For a year after the enactment of the law its effects were not prominent. Pooling was abolished, but the agreements to maintain rates were still kept up and were fairly observed. But in 1888, the second year of the law's working, it came to be realized that the pool was the vital strength of the agreement to maintain rates, and that this agreement might now be easily broken. Then ensued a remarkable season of rate cutting, which, at the present writing, has reduced many strong companies to the verge of bankruptcy. It is plain enough that if this is allowed to go on, the various stages of receivership, sale, and consolidation will follow in regular order. To avoid this too sudden revolution and the general financial disaster which all sudden revolutions entail, the principal companies in the West are now striving to combine in an association for the maintenance of rates by a plan which will bind them more closely together than any other ever before adopted. Thus to quote Mr. Adams again: "The Interstate Commerce law has given a new impetus to the process of gravitation and consolidation, and it is now going on much more rapidly than ever before. It is at this moment rapidly driving us forward toward some grand railroad-trust scheme."

It is a fact which we shall do well to ponder over, that this legislation intended to stimulate competition has finally had just the opposite effect from that which its makers desired. They did increase the intensity of the competition, and have thereby nearly brought about a permanent end to all competition in railway traffic.

It must now be clear that the railway is essentially a monopoly, not, be it noted, because of any especial wickedness of its managers or owners, but because competition is impossible as regards the greater part of its business, and because wherever competition is possible, its effect, as the managers well know, would be to annihilate all profits from the operation of the road.

Let us consider now some of the evils with which this monopoly is charged. The first of these is discrimination between persons and between places. A favored shipper has been enabled to ruin his competitors because he could obtain special rates, while they, perhaps, were charged an extra amount. The strong monopolies have in this way been able to strengthen their hands for the purpose of throttling their weak competitors. Passenger rates, too, have been low to one class and high to another; and the system of free passes has led to great abuses. Discrimination between towns and cities and States has been hardly less serious; and while the railways were permitted to make high local rates and low through rates, a great stimulus was given to the city at the expense of the country. The second class of evils is that rates in themselves have been too high. The railways have been wastefully built and then capitalized at double their actual cost, and it has been attempted to pay dividends of 6 to 10 per cent. on these securities. In some cases the principle of charging "what the traffic will bear" has been so applied that industries have been ruined through the absorption of their profits by unjust transportation charges. But our space will not permit a comprehensive review of the many abuses of railway management. They are already familiar to the public. We needed only to refer to them sufficiently to carry on our argument by showing that the railroad monopoly is not by any means a harmless monopoly if left to work its own pleasure.

There are two evils of our present railway system, however, which are not chargeable to monopoly, but to the attempt to defeat monopoly, and which are important to our discussion. The first is the waste of competition in railway traffic; the second, the waste of competition by the construction and threatened construction of competing lines where present facilities are ample for the traffic. Of the first it need only be said that in advertising, "drumming," and soliciting patronage the railways spend many millions of dollars every year, which comes out of the pockets of the public. The second is most serious, for it involves a far greater waste. It is a conservative estimate to say that 5 per cent. of the railways of the country were only built to divide the profits of older roads, and that their owners would be delighted to-day to have their money back in their possession and the railroad wiped out. The millions these roads have cost, the millions required every year to maintain and operate them, the millions spent on proposed roads that never reached completion, and the millions squandered in fighting proposed roads by every means short of actual bloodshed,--these are some of the wastes which we have made in our endeavor to create competition in railway transportation. And with all our efforts, and notwithstanding the fact that until within a short time the public sentiment and the railway managers have been united in the belief that free competition was the only mode of regulating railroad rates, we are farther removed from free competition now than ever before.

And now consider in addition to all this the fact that every railway company must first of all secure from the State a right to exercise the sovereign power of Eminent Domain, and that it may and does choose and take every advantage of the favorable locations where its road can be built most cheaply; which natural highways, mountain passes, and the like, are gifts of Nature, the right to whose use equitably belongs to the general public, and not to private parties exclusively. Taking these facts also into consideration, it seems needless to offer further proof of the fact that the business of railway transportation is essentially a monopoly, and that the attempt to regulate it by competition must always prove a failure in the future, as it always has in the past.

Necessarily we have limited our discussion to the most salient points, and have not touched at all many of the complicated details of the railway problem. In a later chapter we can study farther the evils due to railway monopolies, and the proper remedies therefor. At present we have accomplished our purpose in finding out the fact that railways are monopolies, and that they are so by their inherent nature.

Of monopolies in other forms of internal transportation, but little need be said. Our once busy canals and great rivers seem destined, with the constant rapid improvement and cheapening in the carriage of goods by rail, to lose all their former importance. The monopolies small and great that once held sway there have all vanished before their strong rival, the railway.

The use of steam in the vessels that navigate the ocean has had an effect very similar to the replacing of stage-coaches and freight wagons by the locomotive. Where hundreds of sailing vessels plied their slow and uncertain trade, steamer lines now make trips only less regular than the railway itself. The only cause for the existence of a monopoly in ocean traffic by steam is the greatly increased capital required for a rival steamship line as compared with that needed for the old sailing vessels. We find this, the requirement of a large capital, to be a feature of more or less importance in nearly every monopoly of the present day. In this case, however, unless there is an artificial monopoly in the shape of government aid or authorization, the strength of its capital is the only power the monopoly has.

We may reach a clear idea of the essential nature of all the monopolies considered in this chapter by considering an especial class of monopolies of communication, namely, mountain passes, bridges, and ship canals. If a person or a railway corporation could secure sole control of the only pass through a high mountain range separating two wealthy and populous districts producing goods of different sorts, they might exact a princely yearly revenue for its use, equal to the interest on the capital required to secure an equally favorable passage by tunnelling, or the annual cost of sending goods over some longer and more expensive route. But under the law no private person would be allowed to do this; and if the pass were a very important and necessary one, probably no one railway company would be allowed to do so. The law recognizes to some extent, and should recognize much more than it does, the fact that the benefit of this natural pathway is not the property of any one man or set of men, but equitably belongs equally to every person who needs to use it directly or remotely.

A very large and expensive bridge is like an important mountain pass, differing only in that one is the gift of Nature, while the other is wholly the work of man. But because the latter is the work of man, it does not follow that it is not a monopoly. The great bridge across the Mississippi River at St. Louis is owned by a private company which levies tolls for the teams and trains passing over it. These are deemed excessive, as they are sufficient to pay an exorbitant interest on the cost of the bridge. Yet for many years no one has cared to invest money in the erection of a new bridge, for they saw that there was no more traffic than one bridge could readily carry, and they knew that if a new bridge were erected, in the rivalry in tolls which would ensue, the old-established company would probably bankrupt its rival. It is thus plainly seen how an important bridge may become a monopoly, and a most powerful and onerous one.

We have still one important monopoly of communication to describe, the telegraph. Viewed from a narrow standpoint it may be thought that there should be no monopoly in the telegraph. A telegraph line is not expensive to erect and maintain, and it gets no monopoly from taking advantage of the most favorable route through difficult country as a railway does. But the economy effected by combination and the effect of sharp competition in bringing about bankruptcy and then consolidation are exactly similar to the case of the railway, which we have just described. In the early history of telegraph companies, many short competing lines struggled and fought for supremacy. In 1859 the Western Union Telegraph Company was formed with the avowed intention of combining these warring companies and making the telegraph business profitable. It has exceeded the most sanguine dreams of its promoters by swallowing up its rivals until the entire system of telegraph communication of the country is practically in its hands. The effects of this consolidation have been of two sorts. On the one hand we have the telegraph service of the country performed with the least possible work; there is nothing wasted in the maintenance of two or more rival offices in small towns where one is sufficient, nor in operating two lines of wire where a single one would serve as well. All expense of "drumming up" business in various ways is avoided, and also the cost of keeping the complicated books necessary when the receipts of a single message must be divided among several companies. On the other hand it is plain that the public is wholly at the mercy of the monopoly in the matter of rates, and must pay for the use of the telegraph exactly what the corporation asks. There is a weak and foolish argument which is often used in an attempt to show that this particular monopoly is not hurtful. It is that the telegraph is a luxury which only wealthy people use, and hence whether its rates are high or low is of little account. The fallacy of this statement is easily seen. A principal use of the telegraph is to aid the prosecution of business; hence to unduly raise rates is to cause an additional tax on business,--on the carrying on of the processes of production. This tax will certainly have its effect, either in decreased profits, decreased wages, or an increased price for the product. Another large class of telegrams are those which are sent with little thought of the cost, in time of sickness, death, or sudden emergency, yet by people whose purse feels severely the tax.

What to do with this vast monopoly is one of the questions of the day, but we will content ourselves at present with this investigation of its character, reserving its proper treatment for later consideration.

V.

MUNICIPAL MONOPOLIES.

The people who live in cities are far more dependent on monopolies than the resident of the country. The farmer can still, on necessity, return to the custom of primitive times, and supply himself with food, clothing, fuel, and shelter without aid from the outside world; but the city dweller must supply all his wants by purchasing, and is absolutely dependent on his fellow-men for the actual necessaries, as well as the luxuries of life. From the peculiar circumstances of city life, many monopolies arise in production and transportation which occur nowhere else. One of these is the carriage of passengers on street and suburban railways. There is no better instance, perhaps, of the great power which is placed in the hands of railway managers than this matter of suburban passenger traffic. One example must suffice to show this. Let us suppose that the managers of a railway, which has hitherto not been run with a view to the development of suburban traffic, secure control of several choice tracts of land on the line of their road near a growing city, and establish low rates of commutation and frequent and convenient train service. The land which they purchased is sold out in building-lots for many times its cost, and a number of thriving villages become established there, inhabited chiefly by people whose business is in the city and who are obliged to go back and forth on the trains. After a number of years the growth of the towns becomes more sluggish, and the managers find that the commutation traffic is not after all extremely profitable; therefore they lessen their train service and increase the rates of fare. Perhaps they may abolish commutation rates altogether. It is a well known fact that the value of suburban real estate depends almost entirely on the convenience and cheapness of access to the city. By the removal and forced sale, which many of these people will be obliged to make, it may easily happen that they may lose their entire property. It is not stated that such flagrant cases of autocracy on the part of railway managers are common. Indeed, it is a high compliment to the uprightness and probity of these men that such occurrences are so infrequent, and that the temptation, so constantly presented, of enriching one's self at the expense of the owners of the road and the public is yielded to so seldom. But there have been cases where railway managers have secured excellent train service and low rates of fare to benefit places where they held an interest in real estate, while other and competing places were given poor service and high rates. And the entire abolition of long-established commutation rates has happened more than once.

But turning now to the city railways proper, those carrying passengers through the streets, it is evident at first sight that we have another case where competition is a factor of little account. The power of this monopoly for harm is greatly intensified by the fact that its use is largely a necessity. In all our great cities the business sections are far removed from the residence sections, and the great mass of the industrial population is obliged to ride at least twice each day in going to and returning from work. In nine cases out of ten there is one route so much more convenient than any other as to overbalance any slight difference of fare. Thus, even on the supposition that every different line was run in competition with every other line, the amount of really competitive business would be but a trifle. But besides this, as is well known, in a great many cities consolidation has gone on as rapidly among street-railway companies as among the great trunk-line railways. The three lines of New

York elevated roads were originally projected by rival companies; but they were not long in coming together under one management. A Philadelphia syndicate has secured control of most of the street railways of that city, and in addition has purchased a number of the lines in Boston, Chicago, Pittsburg, and St. Louis. Although the benefit in economy by consolidation is much less in the case of street railways than in the case of steam roads, yet considerable is gained, and the competition which is killed by the consolidation is, as we have just seen, of no great importance to the public. The so-called street-railway trust, then, is really of no great moment. The monopoly in street-railway traffic arises from the nature of the business rather than from any especial effort of capitalists to kill competition.

But the railway companies are not the only monopolies which have the use of our city streets. Water, gas, and steam pipes beneath the pavements, and wires, either in subways or strung overhead, carrying electricity for street and domestic lighting, telegraph, telephone, and messenger service, are all necessities to our modern civilization.

The absolute necessity of a public water supply, and the practical impossibility in most cases that any competition in the furnishing thereof can be established and maintained, have led, in the case of most of our large cities, to the work of water supply being undertaken by the municipal authorities. But many of our smaller cities have entrusted to private companies the work of furnishing a water supply. While this is a case of real monopoly, yet under the conditions which may be enforced, most of the power for harm is taken away. According to the best plan in vogue, the city sells the franchise for constructing the works to the company who bids to furnish water at the lowest rates under definitely specified conditions, the franchise being sometimes perpetual, but oftener granting to the city at some future date an option for the purchase of the works. It is to be particularly noticed that this is a case in which the administration of an absolute monopoly has been entrusted to private enterprise with excellent results; a fact which may be of use to us in our later investigation.

While the fact was early appreciated that a water supply when once introduced became an absolute necessity, it was not recognized when illuminating gas was first brought into use how important it was to become. Franchises, or more properly permits, for erecting works and laying mains for supplying consumers were given away to hastily formed companies; and even at the present time there are but a few cities (only five in the United States) which own their works and mains for supplying gas. As a matter of course the gas companies saw their advantage. Knowing that gas once introduced was a necessity at almost any price, they made no move toward lowering rates as new and cheaper methods came into vogue and their output and profits increased. The stocks of our gas companies have been swollen by enormous amounts of water, and upon this fictitious capital they have continually paid enormous dividends. At one time there was a great call for competition in the gas business. The public demanded it, and as usual the demand was supplied. Rival companies were organized, and the city authorities made haste to grant them permits for laying their mains in the city streets. A war of rates of course ensued, and lasted till one company gave up the fight and sold out to its rival. The consolidated company promptly increased its stock by at least the amount which had been spent in purchasing and laying this extra and entirely needless set of gas mains. The public has to pay interest on this sum, and suffer besides the damage done to the pavements by tearing up and re-laying.

In at least twenty cities of the United States has this farce been repeated, and in every case with the same result. It is now generally acknowledged that the attempt to regulate the price of gas by competition is unwise and harmful. Prof. E. J. James, of the University of Pennsylvania, in a monograph entitled "The Relation of the Modern Municipality to the Gas Supply," has treated this subject most fully. He describes the experience of cities in England, France, and Germany, where competition has been tried and abandoned, it being found by dear experience that the gas business is necessarily a monopoly. A Congressional Committee, who reported on the application of a rival gas company which proposed to lay mains in the city of Washington, declared that "it is bad policy to permit more than one gas company in the same part of the city." One of the best informed men in the gas business says: "The business is almost outside of the domain of rules governing other enterprises. Competition is so deadly to it that it is impossible for rival companies to occupy the same street without ruin to both, or without consolidation with its attendant double investment, and cheap light is thus rendered an impossibility."

Hon. T. M. Cooley says:

"The supply of public conveniences to a city is usually a monopoly, and the protection of the public against excessive charges is to be found first in the municipal power of control. Except in the very large cities, public policy requires that for supplying light and water there should be but one corporation, because one can perform the service at lower rates than two or more, and in the long run will be sure to do so. In some kinds of business competition will keep corporations within bounds in their charges; in others it will not. When it will not, it may become necessary to legislate upon profits."

Considering it determined, therefore, that the gas industry is a monopoly, let us inquire something of the manner in which this monopoly regulates the prices for its service. According to recent statistics, collected from 683 gas companies in the United States, 148 companies charge $2 per thousand cubic feet, and 145 companies charge $2.50 per thousand. It is thus seen that rates have been fixed to make "even figures," something which does not occur when margins of profit are reduced by competition. The complete table shows this fact more fully as follows:

7 companies charge $1.00 per thousand cubic feet. 32 " " 1.50 " " " " 24 " " 1.75 " " " " 148 " " 2.00 " " " " 57 " " 2.25 " " " " 145 " " 2.50 " " " " 20 companies charge 2.75 per thousand cubic feet. 86 " " 3.00 " " " " 25 " " 3.50 " " " " 19 " " 4.00 " " " " 120 companies charge various other prices per thousand cubic feet.

According to the same authority these companies in 1886 produced 23,050,706,000 cubic feet of gas, for which they received $40,744,673, an average price per M. of $1.76-71/100. According to the statement of good authorities, gas can be manufactured at a cost of 50 to 75 cents per M. in this country. Prof. James, in his work before quoted, says: "In England at the present time gas is manufactured at a net cost of 30 cents per thousand feet; some works in New England now manufacture it for 38 cents per thousand feet to the holder." The President of the American Gas-Light Association is quoted as stating in an address before the Association that the cost of the gas delivered to consumers by the South Metropolitan Company of London in 1883 was 39.65 cents per thousand, and figuring by the relative cost of coal and labor there and here, he stated that gas could be delivered in New York at a cost of 65 cents per thousand. In Germany the price of gas to consumers varies from 61 cents in Cologne to $1.02 in Berlin. Very recent improvements in processes have greatly cheapened the cost of manufacture. Mr. Henry

Woodall, the engineer of the Leeds, England, gas-works, states that coal-gas costs in the holder 22 cents per thousand. Of nineteen companies doing business in principal English cities, the average rate charged consumers is 52?cents, and the average cost of manufacture is 37-1/3 cents.

The history of the gas monopoly is repeating itself in the matter of electric lighting. The smaller cities of the country, in their haste to "boom," are ready to grant a liberal franchise to the first firm or company which offers to supply an electric-lighting system, trusting to future competition to regulate prices, a resource that must prove of no avail. Nor are the men in power in our larger cities any wiser. The city of New York is taking every means to encourage the operation of rival electric-light companies, and is letting yearly contracts for street-lighting to the lowest bidder. It is true that competition is active just now, but it requires no far-seeing eye to discern the inevitable combination and consolidation among the companies.

Again, not only is competition of this sort sure to fail, but the attempt to establish it is very harmful. To say nothing of the expense and waste of wealth which is involved when rival companies are allowed to stretch their wires and establish their extensive central stations in the same district, it is everywhere acknowledged that the multiplication of wires overhead is a crying evil and danger. Are we to double and treble it, then, by permitting rival companies to place their wires wherever they please? It is evident that the temporary rivalry which we obtain in this way is bought at much too great a cost. What is true of electric street light wires is equally true of the vastly greater multitude of wires which belong to our rapidly growing system of domestic lighting, and the telegraph, telephone, and messenger service. Surely no man knoweth the beginning or the end of the network which is woven over our heads, and which, besides all the useful wires already enumerated, is full of "dead" wires, many of them strung by defunct or irresponsible companies, who would never have been allowed to obstruct the streets if they had not been "competing" for the business. Can there be any doubt that it is the height of folly to continue this work, and that the only rational way of entrusting electric service to incorporated companies is to permit but a single company to operate in a district and control prices by some other means than competition?

We have the beginnings of other monopolies in our city economies which are destined to become much more important, but to which we need only refer.

Steam for supplying heat and power is beginning to be distributed from great central stations, through mains laid underground, to all parts of the surrounding district. The necessity for frequent repairs and stoppage of leaks renders it necessary to break the pavement and dig down to the mains much oftener than is required for any other of our underground furniture. Nothing would seem more evident than that the number of these pipes to be laid should be the fewest consistent with the proper supply of the district, yet it is a fact that for a time two competing steam companies were permitted to run riot in the streets of lower New York, until the weaker one succumbed "to over-pressure." Yet it is scarcely to be doubted, that if another rival company were to ask for a permit to operate in the district now monopolized by the New York Steam Company, public opinion would tend to favor the granting of the permit "because it would give more competition." It is to be hoped that before these great systems for the distribution from central stations of various necessities reach much greater proportions, the public will become educated enough to perceive the folly of attempting to regulate them by competition.

The necessity for this will be more, rather than less, apparent with the use of underground instead of overhead wires. The cost of placing wires in subways is far beyond the cost of stringing them on poles, and if we are obliged to build our subways large enough to accommodate all the rival wires which may be offered, we have a herculean task upon our hands.

The great question of the monopoly of land can be merely touched in this connection. While the fact that land is natural wealth must be freely acknowledged, it is only where population is most dense that any great monopoly appears in its ownership. The principle is well established, indeed, that private ownership of land cannot stand in the way of the public good. When a railway is to be built, any man who refuses to sell right of way to the railway company at a reasonable price may have it judicially condemned and taken from him. We have already noted in the chapter on railway monopolies the injustice of permitting a single person or corporation to control and own any especially necessary means of communication, as a mountain pass or a long and expensive bridge, and the same principle is apparent in connection with the railway terminals in our large cities. The enormous expense attendant upon securing right of way for an entrance to the heart of the city, makes it a very difficult matter for any new company to obtain a terminus there, except by securing running rights over the tracks of an older company. To give to any single corporation the sole control of the entrance to a city and permit it to charge what toll it pleases for trains that pass through it, evidently places the city at the mercy of a monopoly. Practically the case is not so bad as this, as most large cities have means of water communication, and the railroads are run to the heart of the city through the public streets. But the time is fast approaching when these city grade crossings will be done away with, and in every city of importance the railways will enter the city on elevated viaducts terminating in a single union depot. Evidently it is contrary to the public welfare to sink more capital in these expensive structures than is necessary; and in general, several companies will use a single structure for entrance and exit. It is evident that the control of these terminals, if vested in a single company, may give rise to just the abuse we have set forth; and that the city itself should retain enough control over its railway terminals and freight-transfer lines to ensure that no single carrier or combination shall monopolize them.

In the last analysis it is evident that the monopoly of entrance to a city is really a monopoly in land, or, we might more properly say, in space. We are fortunate in this country in having millions of acres of land still awaiting cultivation; and while it is not intended here to defend the policy of giving away the estate of the public which our government has pursued, there is no danger for a long time to come that an actual monopoly will exist in agricultural lands. The price of land used for business purposes in a city, however, depends almost wholly upon its location. The price at which a single block of land near Wall Street, in New York City, was recently sold was so great that, at the same price, the value of a square mile would be equal to half the whole estimated wealth of every sort in the United States.

Now the question must occur to every thinking man, by what right does the owner of this property receive this enormous wealth? To make the case of those who advocate the public control of the gifts of Nature more clear, let us consider a special case. Suppose a man in an Eastern city chanced to come into possession two-score years ago of a tract of land in what is now Kansas City. We may suppose that he got it by inheritance, or through some chance, and that, except to pay the taxes upon it, he has never given farther attention to it. During all the years of the city's rapid growth he pays no attention to his land and takes no part in furthering the growth of the city. At last, at the height of the real-estate boom, he sells the land, and, whereas it cost him in the first instance a merely nominal sum, perhaps $100, he sells it now for $100,000. This value it has, not because of itself, as is the case with farming lands, but because of its situation in reference to the community around it. In other words, practically the whole value of this land has been given it by the people who have come and built this city around it. It is their labor that has given this property its value, and, in equity, the value should be theirs. A more detailed statement of the arguments for the public control of land incomes cannot be given here. What we are concerned with here is the extent to which land is subject to a monopoly. It appears too evident to require further discussion that, as a general rule, agricultural lands in every section of the country are competing to a greater or less extent with lands in every other section, and that the lands used for business purposes in the cities compete likewise, each city with others neighboring and of similar size, while lands in the same city similarly situated compete with each other.

VI.

MONOPOLIES IN TRADE.

We have now examined the various forces which are destroying competition in the production of goods in our factories, and of raw material from our mines; in the transportation of these goods in their various journeys between the producer and the consumer, and in the supply of the especial needs of the dwellers in our cities.

It is an old and well-worn adage that "competition is the life of trade"; and if this be true, we shall certainly not expect to find the men who are earning their living by the purchase and sale of goods endeavoring to take away the life of their business by restraining or destroying competition. At first sight it seems as if it would be a difficult matter in any case to destroy competition in trade. The buyer and seller of merchandise has no exclusive control over natural wealth; no mine or necessary channel of transportation is under his direction; nor does he in his trade produce any thing, as does the manufacturer. He only serves the public by acting the part of a reservoir to equalize and facilitate the flow between the consumers and producers; and if necessity requires, the two can deal directly with each other and leave him out altogether. But in dealing with the question of monopolies we must not conclude that the absolute control of supply is at all necessary to the existence of a monopoly. While there are monopolies, as we have seen, which have the keys to some of the necessities of civilized life, there are others which control merely some easier means for their production, carriage, or distribution; and to this latter class belong the principal monopolies in trade. To be sure that this constitutes a monopoly, we have but to turn to the case of the mountain pass mentioned in a former chapter. The use of that particular pass for transporting goods is only an easier means of transportation than the detour to some other pass or by some other route; and the degree of power of the monopoly depends directly on the amount which is saved by the use of its facilities. So with the monopolies in trade. Brokers and jobbers and retail merchants form a channel through which trade is accustomed to pass, and through which it can pass more readily than by any new one.

It is to be noted that under modern conditions the power of middle-men has been greatly reduced from what it was formerly. As we have already seen, manufacturing was then carried on only in families and small workshops, and the mines which were worked were principally in the hands of the king. The merchants were the wealthy men of olden time. They controlled largely the transportation facilities of that day; and while, as we have already noted, the commerce which then existed was but a trifle compared with the present, the principal exchange being in local communities, yet the trade in all articles which were imported, and all domestic commerce between points any great distance apart was in the hands of the merchants.

It is natural, therefore, that we find monopolies in trade to have been among the first which existed and to have been of importance and power when manufacturers' trusts were not dreamed of. The guilds which flourished near the close of the Middle Ages, while not devoted to the establishment of a monopoly, did nevertheless aim, in some cases at least, to hinder competition from those outside their guild.

But turning to the present, let us examine the conditions under which competition in trade is checked to-day. Let us take, first, the case of retail trade in any of the thousands of country villages and petty trade centres in the land. The history of the life of the country store-keeper is a constant succession of combinations and agreements with his rivals, interleaved with periods of "running," when, in a fit of spite, he sells kerosene and sugar below cost, and, to make future prices seem consistent, marks down new calico as "shop-worn--for half price." It is true the sum involved in each case is a petty one, but when we consider the enormous volume of goods which is distributed through these channels, the total effect of the monopoly in raising the cost of goods to the consumer must approach that effected by monopolies of much wider fame. But perhaps it may not seem evident that this is a monopoly of the same nature (not of the same degree) as a manufacturers' trust or a railroad pool. It certainly seems to be true that the merchant has a right to do as he chooses with his own property; and that if he and his neighbor over the way agree to charge uniform prices for their goods, it is no one's business but their own. And, indeed, we are not yet ready to take up the question of right and wrong in this matter. That the act is essentially a "combination in restriction of competition," however, is self-evident. The degree of this monopoly may vary widely. If the merchants who effect this combination raise their prices far above what will secure them a fair profit on the capital invested in their business, and if it is difficult for their customers to reach any other source of supply outside of the combination, the monopoly will have considerable power. On the other hand, if the stores of another village are easy of access, or if the merchants who form the combination fix their prices at no exorbitant point, the effect of the monopoly may be very slight indeed.

We find this class of trade monopolies most powerful and effective on the frontier. Wherever railroad communication is easy and cheap the tradesmen of different towns--between whom combinations are seldom formed--compete with each other. The extension of postal, express, and railway-freight facilities to all parts of the country, too, have made it possible for country buyers to purchase in the cities, if necessary. Thus the railways have been a chief instrument in lessening the power of this species of monopoly in country retail trade, which was of great power and importance a half century ago.

Of retail trade in the cities, it is not necessary to speak at length. Combination here has seldom been found practicable because of the great number of competing units. There is, however, a noticeable tendency of late to the concentration of the trade in large establishments, which by their prestige and capital are able to take away business from their smaller competitors. It does not seem likely, however, that this movement will result in any very injurious monopoly among city retailers.

The wholesale trade is on quite a different basis from the retail. The number of competitors being so much less, combination is vastly easier. The tendency toward it has been greatly fostered and strengthened by the formation of trusts among the producers. These combinations made the manufacturer more independent in his treatment of jobbers, and disposed him to cut their profits to the lowest point. Naturally these men combined to resist this encroachment on their income. They refused to handle any goods for less than a certain minimum commission. It might be possible in many cases for manufacturers to sell directly to the retail traders, but in general the difficulty of changing old commercial channels is such that the friction and expense is less if the goods are permitted to pass through the wholesaler's hands. It is to be noted that one cause for ill-feeling between manufacturer and wholesaler is the fact that before the days of trusts the latter often reaped much greater proportionate profits than the producer himself. But in time this cause of dissension will be forgotten, and the trust and the wholesalers' association will work in harmony.

The point of greatest interest in this is the fact that combinations among this first class of middlemen are fostered and made possible by the combination of producers. Nor does the series end here necessarily. The increased price which the retail dealers are obliged to pay for the goods, with the fact that others are making larger profits, makes them eager to do the same; and by the aid and co-operation of the wholesale merchants they may be able to do much toward checking competition among themselves and increasing their profits. Thus by the operation of the combination at the fountain-head among the producers, there is a tendency to check competition all along the line, and grant to each handler of the goods between producer and consumer an abnormal profit. An excellent example of this is found in the sugar trade. The wholesale Grocers' Guild of Canada, which includes 96 per cent. of the Dominion's wholesale traders, entered into a compact with the Canadian sugar refiners, who agreed that dealers outside of the guild should be charged 30 cents per 100 pounds more for sugar than those who were in the guild. In November, 1887, fourteen members of the guild were expelled and were compelled to pay the higher price. The executive committee of the guild fixed the selling price for the retail dealers. The guild was so successful with sugar that it extended its operations to starch, baking powder, and tobacco, fixing prices for those goods as well. The committee of the Dominion Parliament, appointed to investigate the guild, reported that it was a combination obnoxious to public interest, because it limited competition, advanced prices, and treated with gross injustice those in the trade who were not its members. In New York State there are two associations of wholesale grocers which are working to prevent competition in the sugar trade. They have fixed a uniform price for sugar, and have tried to make arrangements with the managers of the sugar trust by which that organization shall discriminate against all grocers who are not members of the association by refusing to sell them sugar or charging them a higher price. In some other sections an attempt has been, or is being, made by which the retail grocer sells only at certain fixed prices determined by a committee of the wholesalers who issue each week a card of rates. It is urged in defense of the movement that sugar has been sold at an actual loss by both the wholesale and retail trade for a very long time. The Grocers' Association, at its first meeting, passed a resolution declaring that it was opposed to combinations for the purpose of extorting unreasonable profits from the public, and that all that was sought was to prevent the evil of handling certain staples below the cost of doing the business. But if we inquire why these staples have been handled at a loss, the answer is, because of the strong competition which has prevailed. The organization, then, is a combination to limit competition, to suppress it, in fact, and the difference between its purpose and work and that of the Sugar Trust is a difference of degree and not of kind. The reason for its moderate demands may be because grocers are more liberal-hearted than refiners, or because they understand that their power over the trade is more limited than those who control the original product, so that an attempt to exact too large profits would offer a tempting premium to competitors of the Association.

Another staple article of consumption in which combinations are known to exist is meat. It is affirmed that a combine of buyers and slaughterers controls the markets of Chicago and Kansas City, and both depresses the price paid for cattle in the market, and raises the price of beef to the retail dealer. This monopoly proved so oppressive, and attracted so much attention, that in February, 1889, Gov. Humphrey of Kansas, called a convention of delegates from the legislatures of ten different States and Territories to devise a system of legislation, to be recommended for adoption by the several States, which should destroy the power of the combination.

One of the combinations investigated by the New York State Committee appointed to investigate trusts and similar organizations, was an association of the retail butchers, and the brokers buying sheep, lambs, calves, etc., from the farmers. The purpose of the association is to prevent competition among its members and keep control of prices in its own hands by charging a higher price to outsiders than to members of the association. The ultimate effect is to increase profits by paying less for the animals and getting higher prices for the meat sold.

We might go on at indefinite length to examine the various monopolies of this sort, but it does not seem necessary. The salient fact which is evident to any one at all conversant with business affairs is, that in almost every line of trade the restriction of competition is in force to a greater or less extent. Those monopolies are strongest, indeed, which have control of production; but in so far as they can control the market, the men engaged in buying and selling are equally ready to create minor monopolies, and an acquaintance with the general markets convinces one that these monopolies are numerous enough to have a very important effect in increasing the cost of goods to the consumer.

We are accustomed to think of competition as a force which always tends to keep prices down, and of a monopoly as always raising prices; but it should be understood that this is true only of the competition and monopolies among sellers of goods. It must be remembered that the competition among buyers, is a force which acts in the opposite direction and tends to raise prices; and that it is quite possible to have combinations among buyers to restrict competition and keep prices down. Of course, where the buyer is the final consumer, this is almost impossible, for the great number of competitors forbids any permanent combination. Also where the product concerned is a manufactured article or a mineral product, the mining or manufacturing company or firm will generally have capital enough and business ability enough to defeat any attempt of the wholesale merchants to combine to reduce the prices paid for their output. This he can easily do by selling to retail dealers direct. But in the case of products gathered from the farmers the case is different, and the producer can less easily protect himself against combinations among buyers to fix the price he shall receive. The power and extent of these monopolies varies with the distance of the farmer from markets, and also, it must be said, with the intelligence and shrewdness of the farmer. In districts remote from railways and markets the farmers are often dependent on the travelling buyers for a chance to sell their cattle or produce. In a thinly settled region there may be no more than two or three times in a season when a farmer will have an opportunity to dispose of his surplus products; and, realizing his necessity, he is apt to be beaten down to a much lower price than the buyer would have given if other buyers had been competing with him to secure the goods. In the chief markets, too, there is often a combination of buyers formed to keep down prices. The combine of cattle-buyers in Kansas City and Chicago has just been noted. The New York Legislative Committee discovered that a milk trust had control of the supply of milk for New York City, fixing the price paid to the farmer at three cents per quart, and the selling price at 7 or 8 cents per quart. According to the suit brought by the Attorney-General of Louisiana against the Cotton-Seed Oil Trust, that monopoly has reduced the price paid to the planters for seed from $7 to $4 per ton. As the total amount of cotton seed which it purchases is about 700,000 tons a year, it is evident that this feature of the combination alone puts into the pockets of the owners of the Trust over two million dollars per annum, over and above the profits made through its control of the cotton-seed oil market. Evidently the combinations which lower prices by restricting competition among purchasers are not to be overlooked because of unimportance.

In the chapter on monopolies of mineral wealth it was stated that the French copper syndicate is not a "trust," but a "corner." It has not been common to consider "corners" as a species of monopoly, except as they have, like the latter, acquired a bad reputation with the general public from their effect in raising the price of the necessaries of life. But if we look at the matter carefully, it becomes plain that the aim of the maker of corners is the same exactly as that of the organizer of trusts,--to kill competition. The difference lies in the fact that the "corner" is a temporary monopoly, while the trust is a permanent one. The man who forms a corner in, let us say, wheat, first purchases or secures the control of the whole available supply of wheat, or as near the whole supply as he can. In addition to this he purchases more than is really within reach of the market, by buying "futures," or making contracts with others who agree to deliver him wheat at some future time. Of course he aims to secure the greater part of his wheat quietly, at low figures; but after he deems that the supply is nearly within his control, he spreads the news that there is a "corner" in the market, and buys openly all the wheat he can, offering larger and larger prices, until he raises the price sufficiently high to suit him. Now the men who have contracted to deliver wheat to him at this date are at his mercy. They must buy their wheat of him at whatever price he chooses to ask, and deliver it as soon as purchased, in order to fulfil their contracts. Meanwhile mills must be kept in operation, and the millers have to pay an increased price for wheat; they charge the bakers a higher price for flour, and the bakers raise the price of bread. Thus is told by the hungry mouths in the poor man's home, the last act in the tragedy of the "corner."

Fourier tells of an event in his early life which made a lasting impression on him. While in the employ of a mercantile firm at Marseilles, his employers engaged in a speculation in rice. They purchased almost all the available supply and held it at high prices during the prevalence of a famine. Some cargoes which were stored on shipboard rotted, and Fourier had to superintend the work of throwing the wasted grain, for the want of which people had been dying like dogs, into the sea. The "corners" of the present day are no less productive of discontent with the existing state of society than were those of Fourier's time.

But, returning to our subject, it should be said that the "corner," generally speaking, does much less injury to the public than is commonly supposed. As we have shown, the manipulators of the corner make their chief profits from other speculators who operate on the opposing side of the market; and it is but a small part of their gains which is taken from the consumers. The effect on the consumer of the abnormal rise in price caused by the corner is sometimes quite made up for by the abnormal fall which occurs when the corner breaks. Generally, however, the drop in prices will be slower to reach down to the final consumer, past the middlemen, than will the higher prices. The corner makers also are apt, if they are shrewd and successful, to make the total of their sales for the current supply yield them a profit. Thus suppose that the normal price of wheat is 70 cents per bushel, and that the syndicate secures control of five million bushels at the normal price. If while it keeps the price up it sells two million bushels at $1.20 per bushel, it can afford to get rid of the rest of its stock at an average price as low even as 50 cents per bushel, and still make four hundred thousand dollars' profit.

The operations of corner makers are confined principally to goods which are dealt in upon commercial exchanges. One evident reason for this is that the vast purchases and sales, which are necessary in the formation of a corner are impossible without the facilities afforded by an exchange. It must be said, too, that the plain truth is that our principal commercial exchanges, while they do serve certain useful purposes, are yet practically devoted chiefly to speculation. This, simmered down to its essence, means that the business of the speculators is to bet on the future prices of the articles dealt in,--a game in which the largest players are able to influence prices to accord with their bets, and hence have their "lamb" opponents at an obvious disadvantage. The evil of this sort of commercial gambling is recognized by practical men of every class; but its cure is yet to be effected.

A sort of business allied both to trade and transportation is the business of storage or warehousing, and this has recently shown some interesting cases of monopoly.

The owners of warehouses along the Brooklyn waterfront combined their business in January, 1888, and doubled their rates for storage. In the testimony of one of the members of this trust, before the New York Legislative Committee, he said: "We want to destroy competition all we can. It is a bad thing." The owners of grain elevators at Buffalo, N. Y., have long combined to exact higher prices for the transfer of grain than would have prevailed were free competition the rule. At the session of 1887 the New York Legislature took the bull by the horns and enacted a law fixing a maximum rate for elevator charges; a statute which was based on the popular demand for its enactment, but is hard to accord with the principles of a free government.

There are a number of lines of business auxiliary to trade in which competition is more or less restricted by the fact that the amount of capital controlled and the prestige of the established firms renders it a difficult and risky matter to start a new and competing firm. The insurer of property or life, if he be wise, will demand financial stability as a first requisite for the company in which he takes a policy. The companies engaged in the business of fire insurance have long been trying to agree on some uniform standard of rates and the avoidance of all competition with each other. These combinations, however, are apt to be broken, as soon as formed, by the weaker companies, whose financial condition operates to prevent them from getting their share of the business under uniform rates. Even when this rate-cutting is stopped, there is still competition to be met from the various small mutual companies, who are necessarily outside the combination.

Banks are a necessity to the carrying on of modern commerce, and they have great power over the financial affairs of the business men of the community which they serve. As a general rule, however, they are largely owned by the merchants and others who patronize them, and the instances of this power being abused are, therefore, not common. It is to be remembered, in discussing this, as in other monopolies, that the power of a monopoly depends entirely upon its degree. A bank, trust company, or real-estate guaranty company which has a great capital, an established reputation for safety and conservatism, sole control of many special facilities, and conveniences for obtaining and dispatching business, has a real monopoly, whose degree varies with the tendency people have to patronize it instead of some weaker competitor, if one exists. There is no evil effect from the monopoly upon the community, unless it takes advantage of its power to charge a sum greater than their real worth for the services it renders, or uses it to discriminate to the injury of special persons or places.

In closing our discussion of the monopolies in trade, there is an important point to be noted. In the lines of industry considered in the preceding chapter, the monopoly was easy of maintenance because it held full control of the source of production, or of some necessary channel through which commerce must pass. No gift of nature assists to maintain a monopoly in trade. It must be wholly artificial, and it relies for its strength simply on the adherence of its members to their agreement to maintain prices. Its degree of power can never be great, compared with monopolies which control the original sources of production; for if it is attempted to put up prices inordinately, competition will start up outside of the combination, or the consumer will be led to deal directly with the producer.

Because of this weakness, the temptation is great for these monopolies to strengthen themselves in ways quite indefensible on any score. The alliance of trade monopolies with trusts, in order to strengthen themselves, we have already considered. But the trust which makes such an alliance must plead guilty to the charge of discrimination as well as monopoly. It is bad enough to raise the prices of the necessaries of life, and force the whole community to pay the tax; but it is worse to add to this the crime of discrimination against certain persons in the community, at the instance of a minor monopoly.

But the trade monopoly does not confine its sins to tempting the stronger monopoly to practise discriminations. It practises discrimination itself in some very ugly forms. A combination among manufacturers of railway car-springs, which wished to ruin an independent competitor, not only agreed with the American Steel Association that the independent company should be charged

$10 per ton more for steel than the members of the combine, but raised a fund to be used as follows: When the independent company made a bid on a contract for springs, one of the members of the trust was authorized to underbid at a price which would incur a loss, which was to be paid for out of the fund. In this way the competing company was to be driven out of business. It is often argued that combinations to advance prices can never exist long, because of the premium which the advanced price puts upon the entrance to the field of new competitors; but the weapons which this trust used to ruin an old and strong competitor are even more effectual against a new-comer; and the knowledge that they are to meet such a warfare is apt to deter new competitors from entering the field.

The boycott was once deemed rather a degrading weapon of warfare; but now the term has grown to be a familiar one in trade circles. Even the great railway companies do not scruple to use the boycott in fighting their battles. One might imagine that both the thing and the name filled a long felt want.

VII.

MONOPOLIES DEPENDING ON THE GOVERNMENT.

The fact has been already referred to that the principal monopolies which existed previous to the present century were those created by government. In the days when governments were less strong than now, and less able to raise money by such taxes as they chose to assess, it was a very convenient way to replenish the king's exchequer to sell the monopoly of a certain trade to some rich merchant. Nor was the establishment of these monopolies entirely without just reason. In those days of scarce and timid capital, inducements had to be held out to encourage the establishment of new enterprises. An instance of this, familiar to every one, was the grant to the owners of the first steamboat of the sole right to navigate the Hudson River by steam for a term of years. In the early history of the nation and in colonial days, government grants to establish local monopolies were very common. In this, however, we only followed the example of the mother country, which had long granted limited monopolies in trade and transportation as a means of encouraging new enterprises and the investment of capital.

The monopolies of the present day which are properly considered as government monopolies are of two classes. The essential principle on which all are based is that their establishment is for the common benefit, real or supposed; but the first class--to which belong the patents and copyrights--are also justified on the ground that the brain worker should be protected in his right to reap the just profits from his labor.

The effect of a copyright is simply to make it possible for an author to receive some recompense from his work. He can only do this by selling it in printed form to those who may wish to buy; but if there were no copyright, any printer might sell duplicates of the book as soon as it was issued, and could sell them at a much less price than the original edition, as the book would have cost him nothing to prepare. The practical result would thus be that few could afford to spend study and research in writing books, and the volumes which would be printed would be apt to be only those of so cheap and worthless a sort that no one would take the trouble to copy them. The monopoly produced by a copyright takes nothing from the public which it previously enjoyed. The writer of a book creates something which did not before exist; and if people do not wish to buy that which he has created, they are at perfect liberty not to do so. The monopoly relates only to the production and sale of that particular book. Others are at liberty to write similar books upon the same subject, which will compete with the first; and the same information may be given in different words without infringing the copyright.

It seems clear enough, then, that the monopoly which occurs in the use of a copyright, is of an entirely different sort from the monopolies which we have previously considered. Competition is not destroyed by it, and its only effect upon the public relates to an entirely new production, which is not a necessity, and which the public could not have had an opportunity to enjoy if the copyright law had not made it possible for the author to write the book with the prospect of being repaid for his labor by the sale of the printed volume.

As already stated, the granting of patents is based on the same principle as the granting of copyrights. A clause of the Constitution empowers the general government to grant to authors and inventors for limited periods the exclusive right to their respective writings and discoveries.

If we judge the granting of patents by the aims and intentions which are held in the theory of the law, we must conclude that it is a highly wise, just, and beneficial act. The man who invents a new machine or device which benefits the public by making easier or cheaper some industrial operation, performs a valuable service to the world. But he can receive no reward for this service, if any one is at liberty to make and sell the new machine he has invented; and unless the patent laws gave him the power to repay himself for the labor and expense of planning and designing his new device, it is altogether probable that he would not spend his time in inventing.

The wealth which a valuable patent promises has been a great incentive to the work of inventors, and has undoubtedly been a chief cause of the great mechanical advancement of the last half century. But the state of mechanical science has greatly changed from what it was when the clause of the Constitution was penned which speaks of inventions as "discoveries." The trained mechanical designer now perfects a machine to do a given work, with almost the same certainty that it will be successful in its operation that he would feel if the machine were an old and familiar one. The successful inventor is no longer an alchemist groping in the dark. His task is simply to accomplish certain results with certain known means at his disposal and certain well-understood scientific principles to guide him in his work. But this statement, too, must be qualified. There are still inventions made which are the result of a happy inspiration as well as of direct design. Not all the principles of mechanical science and the modes of reaching desired ends are yet known or appreciated by even the best mechanical engineers. There is still room for inventors whose rights should be protected. The interpreters of our patent laws have always held the theory that the use of a natural agent or principle could not be the subject of a patent. This is undoubtedly wise and just. The distinction should always be sharply drawn between those existing forces of nature which are as truly common property as air and sunlight, and the tool or device invented to aid in their use.

Again, it is a notorious fact that the great multiplicity of inventions has made the search to determine the novelty of any article submitted for a patent for the most part a farce. No one is competent nowadays to say surely of any ordinary mechanical device that it is absolutely new. The bulky volumes of Patent-Office reports are for the most part a hodge-podge of crude ideas, repeated over and over again under different names, with just enough valuable matter, in the shape of the inventions of practical mechanical designers and educated inventors, to save the volumes from being an entire waste of paper and ink.

Space, however, will not permit us to discuss at length the faults of our patent system. The important point for us to notice is that the patent system establishes certain monopolies, and that these monopolies are not always harmless. Patents are given to "promote the useful arts," but the inventor whom they are supposed to encourage reaps but a small share of the profits of his inventions. Valuable improvements soon fall into the hands of large companies, who are able to defend them in the courts, and reap all possible profits by their use.

Again, patents sometimes aid in the formation of trusts and combinations. Two or three firms may control all the valuable patents in connection with some important industry. If they agree to combine their interests and work in harmony, they are far stronger than an ordinary trust, because the patents they hold prevent outside competition. It was pointed out in the opening chapter how the control of patents was sometimes a feature helping to induce the formation of trusts. The Standard Oil Trust had its origin in the superiority which one firm gained over its competitors through the control of an important patent. The envelope trust, which, at this date, has raised the price of envelopes about twenty per cent., owes its chief strength to its control of patents on the machines for making the envelopes. Instances innumerable could be given where a few manufacturers, who by their ownership of patents controlled the whole field, have ended a fierce competition by consolidating or agreeing to work together harmoniously in the matter of selling-prices. Very many of these are monopolies in trade or monopolies in manufacturing, and as such have already been considered in the preceding chapters; but it is proper here to point out the part which our patent system has taken in their formation, and the fact that it is due to their control of patents that many of the existing combinations owe their security against outside competition.

Probably the public was never so forcibly reminded of the defects of our patent system by any other means as it has been by the operation of the Bell Telephone monopoly. The purpose in granting patents is to aid in the establishment of new lines of industrial activity, secure to the inventor the right to reap a reward for his work, and encourage other inventors to persevere in their search for new improvements. All these things are effected by the monopoly which is held by the Bell Telephone Company; but they are effected at a cost to the users of the telephone under which they have grown very restive. Passing by the statement that the patents which the Bell company holds were illegally procured in the first place, through the inventor having had access to the secret records in the Patent Office of other inventions for which a patent had been asked at about the same time as his own, it is an undisputed fact that the Bell company holds the monopoly of communication by electric telephone in this country. They have managed this monopoly with great skill. While the instrument was yet in its introductory stage, and when every smart town felt obliged to start a telephone exchange or fall behind the times, prices were kept low; but when once the telephone became a business necessity and its benefits were well known, rates of rental were advanced to the point where the greatest possible profits would accrue to the Bell company's stockholders. This was excellent generalship. The same principle is applied in many other lines of business; and it was only because the company held a monopoly of a most valuable industry, that it proved so immensely profitable here. But other acts of the company, it is alleged, while within the letter of the law, are yet clearly infringements on the just rights of the public. It is charged that the company has purposely refrained from putting into practical use any of the many improvements which have been made in the telephone during the past few years, but at the same time has quietly secured their control. By skilfully managing "interferences" of one patent against another, and by amending and altering the various specifications, it contrives to delay as long as possible the issue of the patents upon these inventions. By means of these improvements, which it purposes to introduce as its present patents expire, it proposes to continue its monopoly for many years to come. It is very likely that this attempt will succeed.

We have already seen the folly of establishing competing electric light companies, and the attempt to establish rival telephone exchanges is just as sure to result ultimately in a heavy additional tax on the public. Then, too, the monopoly has grown so wealthy and powerful through its enormous profits that it will be very loth to release its hold, even when it is no longer protected by patents. Rival companies which may be established then, it will seek to crush by a fierce competition; and it will be quite likely to succeed. But in so far as it is not protected by patents, it is properly to be considered with other municipal monopolies, in which class we have already referred to it.

The course pursued by the Bell Telephone Company has at least proved that our whole patent system demands a thorough and radical revision. The inventor should certainly be protected, but not to the public hurt.

The second class of monopolies which the government establishes or aids in establishing because it is deemed to be for the public welfare that they exist, are, first, those private industries which receive aid from the government, either directly by subsidies or indirectly by the taxation of the goods of foreign competitors; and second, those branches of industry which are carried on by the government itself.

The question concerning the granting of subsidies is principally a past issue. A century ago many new enterprises in all lines of industry looked to the government for aid. In those days, when capital was scarce and when investors hesitated at risk, it was perhaps wise to grant the help of the public treasury to aid the establishment of young industries; but nowadays, when millions of capital are ready to seize every opportunity for profitable investment, it is recognized that subsidies by the general government are no longer needed. The days of subsidy granting ended none too soon. The people of the United States gave away millions of acres of their fertile lands and other millions of hard-earned dollars to aid in the building of the railroad lines of the West; and a great part of the wealth thus lavished has been gathered into the coffers of a few dozen men. The monopolies created by these subsidies have been largely shorn of their power; but while they reigned supreme, their profits were gathered with no halting hand.

There is only one direction in which we still hear the granting of subsidies by the general government strongly advocated; that is in the direction of establishing steamship lines to foreign ports. It would be apart from the scope of our subject to discuss the wisdom or folly of such a proceeding farther than to note the fact that it establishes a monopoly.

Take, let us say, the case of a steamer line between New York and Buenos Ayres. It is plain in the first place that the government aid will only be granted if there is not business enough to induce private parties to take up the enterprise. But as we suppose that there was not business enough in the first place to support one steamer line unaided, it is certain that none will undertake to establish a rival line to compete with that already sure of profits by reason of the government aid. Hence this line will have a monopoly of the trade; and unless some proper restrictions as to rates accompany the subsidy, the monopoly may lay an extortionate tax on the public who patronize it.

The relation of the tariff to monopolies is one which deserves the careful attention of every thinking man. Let us, in discussing this question, lay aside all prejudice and preconceived ideas for or against the protective tariff system and consider candidly what are the actual facts of the case. It is evident, in the first place, that the purpose of the tariff tax which the government levies on goods imported from abroad is to keep out foreign competition from our markets. The imported goods cost more by the amount of the tariff than they otherwise would; and the American producer, if he makes equally desirable goods and does not raise his selling price above that at which imported goods can be bought, is secure against foreign competition. But we have already learned that monopoly is simply the absence of competition; and inasmuch as the tariff checks or shuts out foreign competition, it has a tendency toward the establishment of monopoly. But this tendency may not result in the establishment of any monopoly. There is a tariff on potatoes, but there is no monopoly in their production. Evidently the tariff cannot create a monopoly; it only makes its establishment more easy by narrowing the field of competition to the producers of this single country. If we turn back over the list of monopolies we have studied, to find those which the tariff has any effect in aiding to establish, we shall find none till we reach the first two chapters. The monopolies in mineral products and manufactured goods, known generally by the name of trusts, it is self-evident are largely dependent upon the tariff. If they raise their price above a certain point, people will buy goods of foreign production instead. This point--the price at which foreign goods can be profitably sold--depends on the rate of the tariff, on the cost of production in foreign countries, and the cost of their carriage here.

Of the various trusts, it is evident that only those would be effected by the removal or reduction of the tariff whose products are now covered by it. Thus the Standard Oil Trust and the Cotton-Seed Oil Trust would not be injured by any reduction in the tariff. As a matter of fact, however, nearly all of the trusts have to do with manufactured goods which are covered by the tariff, and the two exceptions already named are about the only ones.

The trusts in manufactured products, broadly speaking, then, are all dependent on the tariff. Here is a strange condition of affairs. In the early history of this nation, the people of this country, represented by their popular government, were appealed to by the men engaged in manufacturing after this fashion: "We cannot make the things you need as cheaply as the manufacturers in foreign countries. They are wealthy and we are poor. They have their mills already in operation, we have ours to build. The capital we borrow bears a rate of interest double that which the foreign mill-owner has to pay. The labor we must employ is not yet trained as is theirs, and it must receive far higher wages. Therefore we ask that you aid us in establishing our industries by paying us higher prices for our goods than those for which you could purchase the same goods of foreign manufacture. In order that every one shall be obliged to do this, and that all may contribute equally to our support, we ask you to pass laws laying a tax on all imported goods which compete with ours, whereby none shall be able to buy them at a cheaper price than we can afford to sell our own goods."

And the people replied: "While we recognize the fact that we must pay an increased price for your goods compared with that which is asked for goods from foreign mills, and are thus taxing ourselves for your benefit, yet we see how desirable it is that our industries should be diversified and that we should not be dependent on foreign nations for the necessaries and comforts of life. Thus for a season we will grant your petition and tax ourselves to establish you in your business."

Such was the spirit of the movement that inaugurated the protective tariff. One other great argument for its establishment, which was believed by the people and was assented to by the manufacturers, was as follows: "Our natural advantages for engaging in manufacturing are beyond those of any other nation. Our workmen are more skillful, intelligent, and ingenious; our capitalists are more enterprising. At the same time there are many difficulties to be overcome in establishing a manufacturing business in a new country. Some assistance is needed at the outset to tide it past the critical period. Now, if we can give our manufacturers a start and enable them to establish themselves, they will improve all these natural advantages which we possess; and with the abundance of raw material in our mines and farms and forests, with our ingenuity and Yankee enterprise and skill, who can doubt that our manufacturers, once established, can produce goods more cheaply than they could ever be brought across from foreign countries? This protection from foreign competition will be a great incentive to the establishment of manufacturing enterprises. Everywhere mills and factories will spring up; a brisk home competition will be created; and that will finally reduce prices lower than they could ever go if we remained dependent on foreign countries for our manufactured goods."

It was a wise and well-founded plan, and only as to its final result did it fail. The protective tariff did make manufacturing more profitable than any other business, and mills and factories of every sort have sprung up in all parts of the country. But the expected extreme competition which was to reduce manufacturers' profits and the price of manufactured goods to a basis in accordance with the profits in agricultural and other branches of industry has been long delayed. The wonderful development of the country has kept up prices and profits, and has furnished a market for our manufacturers which has long kept in advance of their capacity to supply it. At last, however, the result which was expected by the founders of the protective tariff has come to pass. Our domestic mills and factories have a capacity beyond the present demand for their products. The home competition which was predicted has come; and if it had operated to reduce prices as was expected, there would now be employment for all our mills, for it is an axiom that every reduction in price increases the demand.

But the manufacturers who had been making enormous profits of ten, twenty, and thirty per cent. on their capital for these many years, were far from willing to accept calmly the situation and reduce their profits to a reasonable figure. They have tried combinations of many sorts to keep up prices, and at last have found in the trust a strong and effective means of killing home competition and keeping up their profits, if they choose, to the highest point which the tariff permits.

It is not to be argued that the manufacturers were especially worse than the general run of men in taking this action. It is the most natural thing in the world that a man who has all his life been used to making enormous profits in his business should come to think that he had an inalienable right to make them; and that when competition became so sharp that he had to lower his prices, it was due to an unnatural condition of affairs glibly designated as "over-production," for which the trust was an appropriate and wise remedy.

It is thus plain how, in a secondary way, the tariff is a cause of the trusts. The fat profits which the former gave have made men covetous enough to engage in the latter.

We are, perhaps, not yet prepared to discuss the question of the proper remedies for trusts; but it is too obvious to call for comment that an easy and most effective remedy is to cut away the protection from foreign competition, under which they flourish, and let them sink or swim as they best can. At the least it will be wise to reduce their protection to a point where any attempt to tax the nation of consumers and reap exorbitant profits by putting up prices so that profits of twenty-five per cent. or more can be reaped, will be counteracted by foreign competition.

It is only fair to point out at the same time that this remedy is far from being a panacea against all trusts and monopolies. The monopolies in the peculiar products of this country will be unaffected by it, and the combinations which embrace the whole globe in their plan of operations are quite beyond its power. The copper syndicate and the salt trust, and according to Mr. Carnegie a steel rail trust, are the only actual examples of international combinations which have ever been attempted, and it will probably be many years yet before the constant movement towards Tennyson's "Federation of the World" permits the general formation of effective industrial combinations which shall embrace all commercial nations.

We have finally to consider the monopolies carried on directly by the government. The carriage of the mails is the most important monopoly carried on by the government, and we may find some facts of interest by enquiring the reasons why it is for the public welfare that it should be so conducted rather than by private enterprise. In the first place, if it were left to private enterprise to furnish us with postal facilities, the postal service would be much more limited than now; many places of small importance being left without postal facilities or charged a much higher rate for service than now. On the other hand--and this is an important point--there would, perhaps, be in and between the large cities competition between different companies; in which case there would be duplicate sets of postal facilities, including buildings, mail-boxes, furniture, and employees of every grade. It is plain that all this would be a waste. One set of facilities is better for the public than two or three or more, and is ample to carry all the mails. To put another set of men at the work that others are already able to do, is to waste just so much of the working force of the world, as well as the capital necessary to furnish tools and buildings for its use. The matter of rates, too, would vary with the competition. One could never be sure what his postage bill for the coming year was to be. The receipts of the companies would be uncertain, and they would be obliged to pay a high rate of interest on the capital invested in their plant, thus making it necessary for them to charge high rates for their service. The intense competition between rival companies would lead to the bankruptcy of the weaker, and the final result would be the establishment of a single corporation in the control of the whole system. Rates would then be put up to the point where the greatest profit would accrue to the corporation.

Under the existing system, then, we save in cost of service over competing systems under private direction, in that the existing facilities are all made use of. There is no waste by setting two men to do the work of one, or by renting two offices to do the business which one could accommodate, neither is any energy wasted in soliciting business. The capital invested by the government in its plant for carrying on the postal service would bear interest, if the money were borrowed, of not more than two or three per cent. But if a private company borrowed money to carry a similar business, they would have to pay five to seven per cent., which they would have to make up for by charging a higher rate of postage.

Other monopolies which have been carried on by the government are the business of transportation, and the provision of roads, bridges, and canals therefor; monopolies in mining; and in the case of municipal governments, as already noted, the supply of water, gas, and electric service, and street railway transportation.

VIII.

MONOPOLIES IN THE LABOR MARKET.

It should be said at the outset of this chapter that, in a very true sense, practically all men are laborers. That into which a man puts his energy and by which he earns his living, is his labor, whether it be work of the hand or the head. But the labor we are to consider in this chapter is that of the men who work for wages; and we will also make the arbitrary distinction that it is that of the men who work for wages in some branch of manufacturing, mining, trade, or transportation, the great divisions of modern industry which we have thus far considered.

Almost all these monopolies employ large amounts of capital in carrying on their business; and in the popular speech, "monopolist" and "capitalist" are often used interchangeably. It is a very common belief that monopolies are confined to the capitalized industries of production, transportation, and trade, which we have already considered; but we are now confronted by the fact that the wage-workers in the various trades of the country are engaged in exactly the same monopolistic schemes, in which they have exactly the same ends in view as have the monopolists who combine millions of dollars' worth of capital to effect their purposes. On the one hand we have the Standard Oil Trust and the Railroad pools and the hundreds of other capitalistic combinations striving to benefit the producer at the expense of the consumer; while among those whose only capital is their strength and skill, we find the workers in all the various trades, and even some of the lower grades of laborers firmly banded together with the avowed purpose of raising their wages above those which they would receive if competition alone determined the rate. And they are successful, too. Notwithstanding the fact that they deal with tens of thousands of producing units where the combiner of capitalized interests deals with tens, the success achieved by the combinations of labor is quite comparable with that reached by combinations of capital. It speaks volumes for the intelligence and ability of the wage-workers of the present day--yes, and for the growth of the spirit of fraternity; that in the advancement of what they deem a just and righteous cause, they should voluntarily put themselves under discipline and endure patiently the untold hardships of uncounted strikes, often brought on in the unselfish work of aiding their brother laborers against what they deem a common enemy.

The modes in which the combinations of skilled laborers attain their desired ends are akin to those which obtain in a well organized manufacturers' trust. The former allow only a certain number of apprentices to learn their trade. The latter permit the establishment of only such additional mills as shall not unduly increase the market supply. The former fix a standard scale of wages below which no member of the union shall work; the latter fix a minimum price for the goods sold in the market. If there are more laborers in the union than can be employed at the advanced rate of wages, some must be idle. If there are more mills in the trust than the lessened demand for the goods will keep busy, some must be shut down. The trade-union boycotts competing workmen outside its ranks, and stigmatizes them as "scabs." The trusts endeavor to punish every outside manufacturer, sometimes by forcing upon him such a competition as shall cause his ruin; sometimes by means as illegal and criminal as are the riotous acts of a mob of hungry workmen, and far less defensible. But let us not yet bring up the question of relative blame. The main point which must impress every candid observer is that the means employed for the monopolies of capital and the monopolies of labor are identical in principle and motive. Nor are we confined to manufacturers' trusts to show that the spirit of rule or ruin characterizes capital as well as labor. Railroad monopolies, in the words of the president of one of the greatest corporations of the country, "strive eagerly to protect themselves while entirely indifferent as to what shall befall their rivals." How many weak corporations have been deliberately ruined by the cut rates of stronger competitors? If the laborer has "scab" in his vocabulary, has not the railroad manager his "scalper" and "guerilla"?

The close relationship, viewed in many different aspects, of the monopolies of labor and the monopolies in production generally has hardly received the notice its importance deserves. Still, it is an evidence that people are thinking of and discussing the matter when such a writer as W. D. Howells, who is popularly supposed to cater to the tastes of those who have very little in common with the laboring classes, puts into the mouth of one of his characters a defence of workingmen for executing a boycott on a non-union workingman, on the ground that they "did only once just what the big manufacturing trusts do every day."

Perhaps it was never so forcibly realized how thoroughly effective these labor combinations have become, and how completely they hold the country at their mercy, as in the strike of the locomotive engineers on the Chicago, Burlington and Quincy Railroad system in March, 1888. Here were, perhaps two thirds of the men in the country qualified for the responsible and onerous work of running a locomotive engine, firmly banded together to advance their own interests and secure assent to their demands. Granted the will, the courage, the discipline, and it was possible, yes, easy, for them to have obliged the railroads to raise the wages of every engineer in the brotherhood to $10.00 per day, for on a refusal they could have enforced the extreme penalty of bringing down a total paralysis upon the business of the country. It speaks volumes for the good sense, the honesty and moderation of the men and their leaders, that, notwithstanding the fact that their demands were not immoderate, and that the failure which came permanently deprived of a remunerative position a thousand members of their brotherhood, they refrained from the extreme to which they might easily have gone, and permitted themselves to be defeated, when they had the power to have forced a different result.

Organized workers in many trades have the power to force wages much higher than they have done. Would that the Sugar Refineries Company, and some other monopolies of production, were as moderate in their demands upon the public as are the workingmen. But though their demands are in one sense moderate, it is yet true that in so far as they exceed the amount which the laborer would receive when the market for labor is open to free competition, they are the direct result of the artificial monopoly which the laborers have created by their combination, and, in effect, levy a tax upon the community. To illustrate: let us suppose that if every man were permitted to follow the trade of bricklaying who wished to do so, the equilibrium between supply and demand would be found at a rate of wages of $3.00 per day. At that rate, if the price rose, more men would wish to follow the trade and at the same time less people could afford to build houses, thus raising the supply above the demand. If the price fell, some of the men would prefer to work at some other trade and more people would conclude they could afford to build houses. But when the rate, which, without prejudice, we call the natural rate, is at $3.00 per day, suppose the men belonging to the trade form a union and resolve to charge $5.00 a day for their work. Then it is very evident that the cost of building is increased, and every one has to pay more for construction and ask a higher rent to repay himself afterward. Evidently, then, by this action of the bricklayers every man in the trade receives $2.00 more per day for each day's work, which must be paid, directly by their employers, but indirectly by the whole community. It would be easy to prove that the tax on the community when the wages are raised in any trade, affects the whole public as well as those directly employing the workers in that trade; but it seems too plain to require proof. The main point we now wish to show, is that any increase in the wages of labor over that received under ordinary competition must be paid by the community, just as much as any increase in the price of coal, iron, copper, wood, wheat, or any other commodity must be paid by consumers at large. Nor does the injury to the community stop here, by any means. We saw that the advance of prices by the linseed oil trust was an injury to all those who, on that account, were obliged to forego painting; and that it thus caused a further injury to painters, paint-makers, and even those employed in the building trade.

But the increase in the price of the bricklayers' work has results no less important. Not only is injury done to those who build and have to pay more for their buildings, but many are prevented from building on account of the increased cost. If we argue according to a prevalent method, we may say that this reduced activity in the building trade will cause stagnation among allied trades with corresponding loss of employment. Again, as a less number of houses are built, and those which are built are more expensive, rents are certain to rise, which means that the poor man must pay out a still greater part of his earnings for his shelter, or else must put up with poorer and meaner quarters.

It is a strange thing to trace, in connection with this, the history of labor, and see how recent it is that the natural right of a man to sell his services for such a price as he could obtain has been acknowledged. History shows that until modern times, compulsory personal servitude has been in every age and country the lot of a large part of the human race. And when wages began to be paid for service, conditions were not much improved. In England, in the fourteenth century, in the reign of Edward III., a pestilence seriously depopulated the country, and reduced the supply of laborers so much that it was not equal to the demand for labor, and wages began to rise. Laws were therefore enacted that each able-bodied man and woman in the realm, not over three score, "not living in merchandise, nor exercising any craft, nor having of his own whereof to live, nor land about whose tillage he might employ himself, nor serving any other," should be bound to serve at the wages accustomed to be given five years previously. No persons were allowed to pay an advance on these wages, on pain of forfeiting to the Crown double what they had paid. Previous to the fifteenth century, workmen in various occupations were impressed into the service of the king at wages regardless of their will as to the terms and place of employment. Indeed, all through the fifteenth and sixteenth centuries, there were continual attempts to fix the rate of wages arbitrarily by law, and also the hours of labor. These, by one old statute, were decreed to last from 5 A.M. to 7 or 8 P.M.

These acts, and others of similar nature, were intended for the subjugation of laborers and the benefit of the employers of labor. It is only since the era of popular government that legislation for an opposite purpose has come in vogue. Gradually the right of the workingman to have the price of his labor fixed as is the price of other commodities, by the law of supply and demand, came to be recognized, although the progress was pitifully slow. The old ideas of the relation between "master" and "servant" were very tenacious of life, and the substitution of the terms "workman" and "employer" is a change which has taken place in England during the present generation.

It was the petty tyranny and the grinding extortion which the laborers had begun to feel, even though they were far better paid and better treated than their fathers, that caused the formation of the original trade unions. Laborers saw that each was helpless alone, but that combined they were a power which their employers need not despise. The old craft guilds furnished them an example of effective combination among those engaged in the same trade; and as men everywhere in every age, when a common danger or misfortune has confronted them, have come together for mutual help and defence, these ignorant laborers, in violation of stringent statutes, but following blindly their human instincts of self-defence, came together and organized the first trade unions.

The common law has always held trade unions to be "illegal combinations in restraint of trade." Between the reigns of Edward I. and George IV., the common law was affirmed and made more effective by the passage of over thirty acts of Parliament, all intended to abolish the trade unions. In 1800 a stringent law was passed, by which all persons combining to advance their wages or decrease the quantity of their work, or in any way affect or control those who carried on the business in which they were employed, might be committed to jail by a justice for not more than three months, or to work in the house of correction for not more than two months. Not till 1824 was an act passed slightly ameliorating this stringent law, and even then the trade unions remained for the most part secret organizations. At last, in 1871 and 1876, laws were passed under which no person can be prosecuted for conspiracy to commit an act which would not be criminal if committed by him singly; and the trade unions, thus legalized, were taken in common with other benefit societies under the protection of the law.

We have already pointed out the main fact that the chief end and aim of the trade unions is the advancement of wages by securing a monopoly of the supply of labor in some particular trade. It is now fair to explain, as we have for other monopolies, the labor monopoly from the standpoint of the laborer himself.

It is a sound axiom of business that a forced sale is apt to be an unprofitable one to the seller; and that when a man's needs are so great that he is absolutely obliged to sell at any price, he is quite certain not to get the full worth of his goods. Now it is an undeniable fact that the condition of many of the wage-workers of the country approximates to this: They must have food, shelter, and clothing for themselves and their families, and the only thing they can offer in exchange for it is their labor. Suppose an honest and industrious man has some misfortune, as an accident, or illness, and loses employment. When once more able to work, he finds his old place filled and new places hard to find; but at last he finds a mercenary employer who agrees to give him half wages. Disheartened at his prospects, he thinks half a loaf is better than no bread, especially when those dearest to him are hungry, and so takes the place. But his employer takes care that his constant work shall leave him no time to hunt for a better position. Indeed, by a few judicious threats from his employer, the man may be put in terror of losing the pittance he already has, and seeing those dependent on him in absolute starvation. Such cases are amply provided for by the trade union. Ill treatment of any one of its members may be avenged by the organization as a whole, on the principle, whose spirit of fraternity and self-sacrifice all must admire, that "an injury to one is the concern of all." More than this, by means of the benefit feature of the fraternity, the member unfortunate, or in distress, is properly cared for. No member is obliged to feel, when seeking for employment, that his food or shelter is at stake if his attempts fail, and he need never be at the mercy of employers who drive sharp bargains.

It is often charged as an evil of trade-unions interfering with wages, that they tend to bring all their members to the same level, and are opposed to the payment of wages in proportion to the varying abilities of the men working at the same employment. But with unorganized labor, and employers who were none too just in their ideas, it was not uncommon to see the necessity of the laborer, or his inability to drive a good bargain, taken advantage of. Thus the workmen whose necessities were greatest, and who were the most docile and obedient, received lower wages than the men who were not particular whether they were busy or idle, and were inclined to pay more attention to their own rights and prerogatives than to the work for which they were hired. While the tendency toward non-recognition of the varying abilities and ambitions of workmen by the trade unions must be deprecated, it has largely grown from the reform of this worse abuse.

There is another benefit which the organization of labor has effected which may, perhaps, be thought an evil by some, but which every broad and generous man must gratefully recognize as a gain to the whole community; and in a self-governed nation like our own, it is a benefit whose importance it is difficult to over-estimate. This is the maintenance of the laborer's dignity and self-respect. We have but to look back to the times we have already mentioned, to see the laborer hardly better than a dog, a cringing dependent, kicked and beaten on slight pretext, and with almost every vestige of manhood worked and bullied out of him. We have come upon far happier times to-day, and there are few corners of the civilized world where conditions so evil prevail now. But without the organization of labor, the status of workingmen would be much farther removed from what is just and right than it now is. Every employer who is wise and honest, and who has the true spirit of a gentleman, will see that his workmen are treated with the respect that is their just due. Discipline there must be, but it is a wrong view of discipline that makes it consist of oaths and brutal insults delivered according to the prevalent good temper or ugliness of the overseer. Unfortunately, not every man who is placed in authority is wise, honest, and a gentleman. Bodily violence is no longer permitted by law, but too often the curses and insults which are heaped on men with no due cause are a violence which is more severe to many a man than actual cuffs and kicks. No man can take such treatment without resentment, and maintain his dignity and self-respect. Yet in how many places is petty tyranny of this sort still active, and its victims are cowed into submission for fear of taking the bread from their children's mouths.

But the member of a strong labor organization need not be cowed or tamely accept insult. He has the right to resent it, and has the power of his fraternity to support him. He knows this, and his employer knows it. Overseers, big with their importance, and inclined to show it by attacking the self-respect of the men under them are no longer in demand.

It is very unfortunate that many people misconstrue this result of the organization of labor as a move toward the abolition of all social ranks and grades. It is nothing of the kind. Social gradations cannot be created or brushed away by any legislative enactment, or the acts of any single class. The combination of the workmen to secure their right to protect themselves from insult is indeed a movement toward making them better and nobler men, just as the abolition of slavery in all its forms was a move in this direction. But no man is truly free if he is not secure in his right to immunity from personal insult as well as from bodily violence. It is not strange, however, that the workman, conscious of the strength of the fraternity behind him, sometimes grows arrogant and insolent toward those who must necessarily be in authority over him. Unaccustomed for generations past to other government than fear of one sort or other, he is all unused to self-control. But it is hardly possible that this should be a great evil. The body of workmen will, eventually, if not now, refuse to sanction and defend their members in any thing which their innate sense of justice must teach them is wrong. Few workingmen will causelessly ask their brotherhood to undertake the hardships and loss of prestige which accompany a strike. And even when insolence is shown toward employers or overseers, they have at least equal power to resent it, and are not, as was the laborer of a half-century ago, forced to submit to insults with outward humility.

We have already noticed the condition of the laws in reference to the laborer in former times: but the repeal of the laws oppressing the workman, and making him a servant to a master instead of a workman for an employer, has been largely due to the organized efforts of the trade unions. To them, also, we owe the passage of many acts like those for the guarding of machinery in factories, the restrictions upon the employment of child labor, and the proper care for the health, comfort, and convenience of employees in general. It cannot be said that the labor interests have always shown great wisdom in all their advocacy of new legislation, and too many acts, like those in reference to the employment of convict labor, show a lamentable retrogression. On the whole, however, there is every reason to believe that the general course of justice has been aided by the influence of the trade unions--something which can be said of very few special interests for whose benefit our legislatures have enacted laws.

All the above facts we must admit in defence of the organizations which have, to a large degree, killed competition in the labor market. But in defence of the especial action of the labor monopolists in forcing wages up to a point above that which competition alone would determine, there is also much to be said. Those who are unwilling to concede that there is any justice in the claim of the wage-workers that full justice is not yet awarded them, are accustomed to expand on the theme of the improved condition of the laborer over that in which he was a century ago. How this can be taken for argument is a mystery. No one thinks of disputing or diminifying the well-known fact that many workmen of to-day have more comforts than the princes of the Middle Ages. The single point in dispute is this: Of the total wealth which is being produced in the world to-day, is the laborer receiving his fair share? There are not wanting men of judgment and ability who answer this question with a decided No. And the greater share of the blame for this injustice they lay upon the monopolies which we have been discussing. They charge, and they verify their charge with ample and sound testimony, that of the wealth which the united brains, and strength, and skill of the world daily produces, the lion's share is taken by men who render the world no proportionate service. This is partly due to existing laws, which the public is not yet wise enough to better; partly to the inertia of public opinion, which is still prone to cling in many points to the idea of past generations that the workman was necessarily a slave; and partly to the narrow selfishness and grasping ambition of many men in the business world. This is not arguing for the reduction of all to a dead level, as is so often absurdly claimed. It is arguing that the inequalities which exist at the present day are not held securely in place by agreement with the inflexible laws of justice and right. Instead they are abrupt and uneven, and contrary to these laws; and there is great danger that the readjustment, which must inevitably take place to bring them in accord with these laws, will come, not as a gradual change, but as a series of terrible social catastrophes, involving us in a wreck which will require a century of civilization to repair.

Only fanatics preach absolute equality. As men differ in their ability and their power to serve the world, so is it just that the reward which the world metes out to them should differ in like proportion. But if we stretch to the utmost the benefit which we conceive the world to derive from the life of many of its men who reap the richest harvest from its production, we cannot in any way make out that their services are so valuable as to deserve such munificent reward. Indeed, it is not very far from the truth to say of some of our most wealthy men that their wealth was won instead of earned; and many place a much worse term in the place of "won."

The workman sums up his case with the argument that as he is confessedly not getting his just share of the results of his work, he is only getting his due, or part of it, if by combination with his fellows to crush out competition, he is able to put up the price of his labor above the natural rate. Finally, as a last defence for the labor monopolies, he calls attention to the trusts and pools and monopolies which are taxing him at every hand for the necessaries of life, and declares that if he, working on the same principle as the wealthy capitalists, is able to combine his tens of thousands of fellows into an effective monopoly, surely he should not be condemned for following the example of the men who are, or are supposed to be, his social, moral, and intellectual superiors.

Such is the strong case which the labor organizations present in defence of the unions which they have formed to kill competition in the labor market. The investigation we have pursued in the preceding chapters enables us to add to this a statement of the case more comprehensive and striking even, than the narrower views which have preceded. In the chapter on the monopolies in trade, reference was made to the fact that the competition among purchasers tends to keep prices up, just as competition among sellers tends to keep them down. Now labor is a commodity whose price in the market is governed by the same laws of supply and demand that regulate the prices of all other things that are bought and sold. But it has this peculiar difference, that the sellers of labor are many, while the purchasers are few, as compared with the relative proportion of sellers and buyers of goods in general. Then, wherever there is little competition among purchasers of labor, we shall expect to find low wages; and where competition to secure workmen is active, high wages will be the rule. This is so obviously true, in the light of every one's experience, that we need not stop to prove it. Now, in the days when manufacturing was carried on in small workshops, there was a great number of purchasers of labor. The concentration of manufacturing in great establishments where thousands of workmen are employed has lessened the number of employers greatly; has it not also lessened competition among them? It is a well-known fact that in many great industries, as, for instance, the mining of coal or the manufacture of iron, there is one rate of wages paid all through one district, and the employers fix that rate through their associations. The makers of trusts have sometimes defended them, on the ground that they enabled the employer to pay his laborers higher wages; but it is plain that when all the firms in a trade are united in one combination, there can be no competition between them for the employment of labor. They will pay them only such wages as they choose; and the bulk of evidence seems to show that, notwithstanding the vast profits which the monopolies are reaping, they have been far from showing any general disposition to share their profits with their employ 閼. It seems almost unquestionable that we have here the real reason for the extraordinary increase of labor monopolies within the past quarter century. This period has witnessed a rapid growth of consolidation and combination in all our industries, lessening thus the number of employers of labor. The wage-worker found himself confronted with the fact that he was soon to lose entirely the benefit of competition for the purchase of his work, and felt that his only salvation from practical slavery was to prevent the competition between himself and his comrades from forcing his wages down to the starvation point. He met the monopoly that threatened to lower his wages by forming another monopoly that could meet the first on equal terms.

We have given little space in this chapter to the consideration of the limit of the power of labor monopolies; but it is obvious that this is very clearly defined. In the first place, while there are certain attempts at combination among unskilled laborers, and those not working at trades, these attempts cannot, as a general rule, be at all successful. Any man out of employment may be a competitor for the work which they do, and it seems practically impossible that any organization can combine, under effective discipline, even a majority of the workingmen of the country not skilled in a trade. The only ways in which attempts to kill competition in unskilled labor can be successful, then, are by the use of force or the boycott, or similar means, and these can never come into vogue as permanent agents in the world's industry. The labor monopolies which exist, and which promise, if let alone, to enjoy continued success, are principally combinations of the workers in skilled trades, and certain of those employed in manufacturing, mining, trade, and transportation.

IX.

MONOPOLIES AND COMPETITION IN OTHER INDUSTRIES.

As we take a look back over the long list of monopolies which we have investigated in the preceding chapters, the natural thought is that we have considered now the greater part of the industries of the country. Certainly these occupations of manufacturing and trade and transportation, are generally considered as our important industries, and a pretty good share of our legislation and public agitation concerns itself with the welfare of these industries and with the men who are employed in them. But certain questions will naturally arise in the curious mind. Just what proportion of our total working population are employed in these industries; and of that number how many are reaping the profits of the monopoly? What are the remaining occupations of our people, and are the workers in them doing any thing to destroy competition? To the investigation of these matters we will devote the present chapter.

The United States Census Bureau classes the gainful occupations of the people in four great divisions: (1) Agriculture. (2) Professional and Personal Service. (3) Trade and Transportation. (4) Manufacturing, Mining, and Mechanical Industries. The monopolies which we have studied in the preceding chapters are all included in the last two classes. The total number of persons engaged in trade and transportation in the country in 1880 is given as 1,810,256, and the total engaged in manufacturing, mechanical, and mining operations is 3,837,112, or a total of 5,647,368 in all these occupations among which we have found monopolies to exist. Of course the great proportion of the persons included in the above number have no direct interest in the profits of the industries in whose operation they aid. It is, indeed, argued that the manufacturer, miner, or merchant who is making enormous profits, pays, therefore, larger and more generous wages; but it is urged on the other side that while this is true in isolated cases, the general rule holds good that the price of labor is governed by the law of supply and demand; and that, as already pointed out, monopoly among producers means a monopoly among purchasers of labor. Let us now, however, leave out this indirect benefit which may, or may not, accrue to the workmen in these various occupations, and find as nearly as we can the number which are, or can possibly be, directly benefited by the operation of monopolies. Let us deduct from the total of 5,647,368, such classes of persons as it is evident cannot have a direct share in the results of a monopoly and are not engaged as skilled workmen in a trade which has been organized to control competition.

We may certainly deduct the following items from the total:

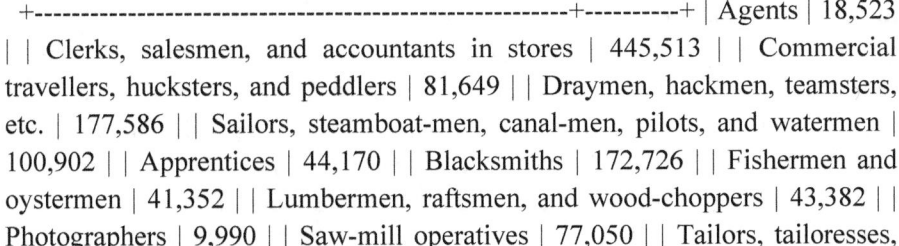

+--+----------+ | Agents | 18,523 | | Clerks, salesmen, and accountants in stores | 445,513 | | Commercial travellers, hucksters, and peddlers | 81,649 | | Draymen, hackmen, teamsters, etc. | 177,586 | | Sailors, steamboat-men, canal-men, pilots, and watermen | 100,902 | | Apprentices | 44,170 | | Blacksmiths | 172,726 | | Fishermen and oystermen | 41,352 | | Lumbermen, raftsmen, and wood-choppers | 43,382 | | Photographers | 9,990 | | Saw-mill operatives | 77,050 | | Tailors, tailoresses,

milliners, and dressmakers | 419,157 | | +----------+ | Total |1,632,000 | +--------
--+----------+

There are a great many other occupations in the list[4] from which these items are taken which might properly be included in the above, as the combination which does or can exist in them it is almost certain is of no practical importance. On the other hand, however, our total of 5,647,368 takes no account of the persons interested in trade, transportation, or manufacturing through holding the shares or bonds of incorporated companies; also the errors and omissions of the census are so great in any event that only broad and general statements can be based upon them. Deducting, then, from the total of 5,647,368 the 1,632,000, which we found to be surely not interested in monopolies, we have about four million persons as the utmost number who are benefited by the profits of the monopolies which we have thus far considered. But let us look into this a little farther. As we have already stated, the monopolies of trade are generally unable to raise prices far above their normal rate. In retail trade, especially, competition shows great tenacity of life. Also with regard to labor monopolies, it is true, as we have already stated, that the limits of their operation are pretty closely defined; even the men in the highest grades of skilled labor cannot secure for each workman by any combination more than two or three dollars per day over what he would receive under the freest competition. Let us, therefore, deduct from the preceding four millions the persons engaged in retail trade, and all skilled laborers in the various trades which we formerly included because we conceived that they might be connected with some form of labor organization, and might also obtain some benefit through the profits of their employers. But when we make these deductions we find that we have only a hundred thousand or so of our four millions left. Briefly summed up, therefore, the fact is, that the strong monopolies in manufacturing, mining, trade, and transportation are owned by a very small portion of the population. Just what this number is, it is impossible to say, for the stock and bonds of railroad companies, mining companies, and manufacturing companies are changing hands continually, and no public record is taken of their distribution and ownership. It may possibly be true, however, that one million different persons own an interest in some of the various monopolies which we have studied, excluding the monopolies in trade and labor. But even if this estimate is correct, it is a well-known fact that a few hundred immensely wealthy men hold a large share of the stock of these very profitable monopolies.

[4] From the "Compendium of the Tenth Census of the United States,"

Part II., pp. 1378 and 1384.

Leaving the questions which this statement opens up, for later consideration, let us consider the other classes of occupations in which men engage for the purpose of gain, and see if this far-reaching movement towards the destruction of competition has infected them, and whether it has proved, or can prove, so successful there as it has in the industries considered in preceding chapters.

The third great class of occupations, rendering professional or personal service, gives employment to over four million persons (4,074,328), and includes in its members those in widely separated ranks of society.

It is, of course, true that the competition in the professions is far more a competition of ability, real or supposed, than it is a competition of price; and the former is a competition which is never likely to be done away with. Yet in all occupations, to a greater or less degree, there tends to arise more or less competition in relation to price, and the professions are not entirely exempt. Lawyers, indeed, seem never to have felt the necessity of fixing any minimum tariff of fees; and so far as is known, clergymen have never combined to advance their salaries. But the medical profession has its well known code of ethics which debars its members from "pushing their business," and has, in certain places and times at least, prescribed a minimum tariff of fees. It should be clearly understood, however, that this is not cited with the intention of putting any aspersion upon the medical profession in any way. The services which are freely rendered to the poor, and the disgusting indecencies and insults which are thrust upon the public by some who choose to ignore this code of medical ethics, would make us ready to forgive very much worse things than a possible tendency among members of the profession to refrain from "cutting under each other" in the matter of fees.

But while the three older professions have evidently little need or disposition to combine for the purpose of increasing their income from the community, some of the newer professions occupy different ground. Architecture is coming to be a profession of no small importance. The principal architects' society, the Association of American Architects, has a regular schedule of minimum commissions below which its members are forbidden to go. Another singular case of professional combination is the Musical Protective Union, a combination of professional musicians in New York City, which fixes minimum prices that its members may charge for their services. On the whole, however, it must be said that the limitation of competition in the professional and intellectual occupations is in this country still in its infancy. In England the fixing of prices of professional service by usage is very much more common, and in many professions the check to competition thus effected is of no small importance. To the careful observer there are indications of a tendency in a similar direction in this country. Is it not more and more common in professional circles to see a slur cast on the man who will work cheaply? There is hardly an occupation or specialty which has not its Associations and its periodicals; and what is more natural than that an association for mutual benefit should come to adopt that certain method of securing mutual benefit at the expense of the public, the restraint of competition?

Examining the remaining occupations in this division, we find that those engaged in them form a large percentage of the whole population. There are of laborers whose occupation is not more definitely specified, 1,859,223. Then there are 1,075,655 domestic servants, 121,942 launderers, 77,413 hotel and restaurant employ 閡, 24,000 soldiers, 14,000 messengers, and enough in other occupations similar to the above, in that very many persons can engage in them without special training, to make it certain that at least three fourths of the members of this division, or a little over three million persons, belong to the class of unskilled workers, among whom, as we have already seen, the attempt to limit competition and force up wages has not, and cannot possibly have, more than a limited and doubtful success. Nevertheless, to a very great extent, the unskilled laborers of the country as well as those working at minor trades are organized for mutual help and protection; and while they cannot increase much the rate of their wages without drawing a host of competitors, they can do much in the way of protecting themselves from injustice and extortion, as we have pointed out in the preceding chapter. It may be possible, indeed, that certain changes in the future, as the requirement of greater skill and efficiency in all kinds of labor, may make combinations in this class of occupations easier and more effective. Our domestic affairs, for instance, are constantly growing more complex, and require greater skill in their operation. Housekeepers are prone to think the "servant girl" problem serious and perplexing enough already. It remains to be seen what they would say if a "Cooks' Protective Union," a "Chambermaids' Sisterhood," or a "Laundresses' Amalgamated Association," should assume control of the wages and hours of labor of their domestics.

To sum up, we find that as a whole the 4,000,000 persons engaged in rendering professional and personal services are in general not increasing the cost to the public of their services by combining together to limit competition; and that so far as we can determine, it is not probable that many of them can do so in the future, even if they are so disposed.

There remains yet one important class of the community to be considered: those engaged in agriculture. Can the farmers of the country fall into line behind the manufacturers and miners and railroad owners, and force up the price of their products by killing competition, to correspond with the increased prices which are demanded in many other lines of industry? They have one thing in their favor in that the principal products of the soil are necessaries of life, which the community cannot do without whether the price be great or small, although an increase in price is sure to result in a decreased consumption.

We may best determine this question by inquiring exactly how the prices are forced up by monopolies. There can be but one way. The laws of supply and demand hold good, and it is out of the power of the producer to greatly affect the demand. It is only the supply of which he has control. From the manufacturers' trust to the laborers' union, the only way in which prices can be controlled is through a reduction in the supply of goods made or men allowed to work; and if the price were to be arbitrarily raised, the result would be the same; there would be a surplus of goods, or some unemployed workmen. In order to raise the price of his products, then, the farmer must do one of two things, which will bring in the end the same result. He must send less of his products to market--lessen the supply--or refuse to sell any thing at less than the increased price which he desires. In either case, if he plants the same acreage and gets the same yield as before, he will have a part of his crop left on his hands.

The query then comes, can it be possible for the farmers all over the country to form so perfect and well-disciplined an organization that every member shall diminish his remittances to market of grain, wool, meat, hay, or what not, enough to raise prices; or that he shall refrain from selling all these articles below a certain defined price? It must be plain to every intelligent person that it would be a practical impossibility to effect such a thing. It would be possible to bring only a small percentage of the farmers in an area 3,000 miles in length and 1,500 in width into a single organization; and it would be essential to the success of this, as of every other scheme, that no outside competition should be permitted to exist.

It may be argued that the Knights of Labor succeeded to a degree in gathering into one organization a large proportion of the workingmen in all the various trades in the country; but their members were mostly in cities, many worked together in great factories, and as regards ease of combination, they were far more easily handled than the widely scattered farmers of the country could hope to be. Besides, the Knights of Labor organization appears to be too unwieldy and cumbrous to be long successful, and internal dissension seems to have already brought it near its end. It is plain that the farmers are powerless to effect a reduction of the competition among themselves. Nor is this condition at all likely to change. Farming is unlike other modern productive industries in that the cost of production does not decrease as it is conducted on a larger scale. The most profitable farms are, and perhaps will always be, the small ones, where the details of the tillage come directly under the eye of the owner.

Such are the facts with respect to the prospect of making a monopoly of agriculture, and it would seem that they are so simple and so easily understood that no attempt would ever be made to restrict competition among farmers. It is to be recorded, however, that such attempts are being seriously made. Prominent farmers of the West in the spring of 1888 took the preliminary steps towards the formation of a farmers' trust. Conventions were held and resolutions adopted reciting that the operation of trusts in manufacturing industries and of monopolies in trade and transportation laid serious burdens on the farmers of the country; and that in order not to be left behind in the struggle for existence the farmers must combine for their own protection. Committees were appointed to work out the details of a plan of organization; but the movement seems to have lost vitality when its projectors came to study it in detail. The preceding argument fully explains the reason.

It should be said, however, that cooperative associations among the farmers are growing at a rapid pace. The Grange and the Farmers' Alliance are primarily cooperative associations for the purpose of benefiting their members in the purchase of goods and in various other directions, and they are fast increasing in numbers and influence. The attempts made to benefit their members in the sale of their produce have been generally confined to protection against the "middle men." The only movement of which the author is aware for restricting production to increase price, has been in certain sections of the South, where recently a general attempt has been made to restrict the acreage planted in tobacco in the hope of raising the price.

It is a matter worthy of note here that the combined influence of the farmers of the country has recently been successful in securing legislation to defeat an important outside competitor. A few years ago some chemists found out that from a cheap substance known as beef suet, an imitation butter could be made, which was in composition and appearance the same as butter made by the ordinary process, and was exactly as nourishing a food. There has been much talk of the halcyon days to come when the progress of science will be so great that food will be made in the laboratory. Well, here was an important practical step in that direction. A cheap product worth three or four cents a pound could be easily converted by a chemical treatment into a valuable food worth three times as much, and the great profit in the business brought this substitute for butter rapidly into use. But at once an indignant protest went up from the farmers of the land. They were being ruined by the competition of the "grease butter" as they disrespectfully called it. There was something suggested about the idea that if just as good butter could be made out of the fat of the cow as out of her milk, and at half the expense, that it would be a benefit to everybody in the country who had butter to buy. But the weak protest for the protection of the general interests of the whole people was not heeded, and Congress passed a bill laying a tax on the new butter sufficient to stop the sale. Here was an evident case of killing competition for the sake of the farming interests, and the force of their unorganized sentiment alone was sufficient to secure the desired legislation. But when the farmers attempt to form a trust, they will have to kill competition among themselves instead of outside competition; and that is a different and far harder matter.

To agricultural laborers the same rule applies which we have found to govern other unskilled labor, viz.: that combination cannot effect much in raising wages. Added to this is the fact that they are widely scattered, and that a great proportion do not follow this as a steady occupation. In England, indeed, there is an agricultural laborers' union, and we may possibly come to that here. But our circumstances are widely different. The fact that in many sections the agricultural laborer is not a "hand," or an "employ?" or "servant," but a "hired man," is an important one, for the difference in terms denote a vast difference in conditions. It is hardly likely that an organization of any sort is to be expected among those in this occupation.

This last division of occupations contains the most members of any of the four divisions. The farmers of the country number 4,225,945 and the farm laborers number 3,323,876. Other minor occupations of the division, as gardener, florist, etc., bring up the total engaged in agriculture to 7,670,493.

We can now make some interesting comparisons. The evident effect of monopoly is, in general, to tax the community at large for the benefit of those who own the monopoly. Let us see what proportion exists between the two classes:

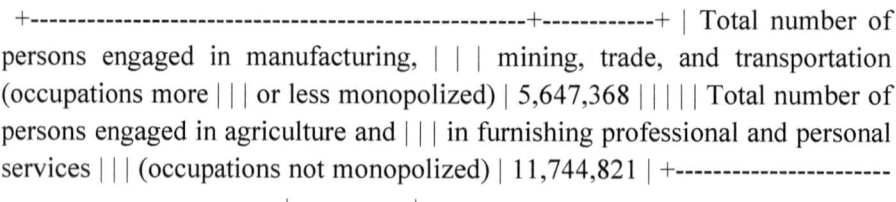

Total number of persons engaged in manufacturing, mining, trade, and transportation (occupations more or less monopolized)	5,647,368
Total number of persons engaged in agriculture and in furnishing professional and personal services (occupations not monopolized)	11,744,821

Thus at the greatest estimate we can make of the number benefited by monopolies, for each man who is gaining by them, two are having their income reduced. If we take the estimate previously made, that the utmost number of persons who can possibly be reaping benefit by ownership of the especially profitable monopolies, trusts, transportation lines, mines, etc., is one million, we have opposed over sixteen millions of the community who are being taxed by their operation. Let a sharp distinction be drawn at this point, however. The above comparison is to be confined to the things between which it is made, and not confused with others to which it has no reference. It is not a comparison of the sort which social agitators are fond of making between the great numbers of the working classes and the relative scarcity of the wealthy. Except so far as the operation of profitable monopolies by the few tends to bring about this unequal distribution of wealth, that is a matter with which we have nothing now to do.

There is one point in this connection, however, which it is well to make plain, as it concerns a class of people which is not included in either of the four divisions that we have already described--those who live on the income of their property.

We have before alluded to the fact that in the popular speech "capitalist" and "monopolist" are often used interchangeably. If we carefully consider the real status of the capitalist, however, we find that of the three requisites of production--labor, capital, and natural agents--capital is the requisite which is most perfectly secured from the control of monopoly. The rate of interest for the use of capital is regulated so perfectly by the law of supply and demand, that all the anti-usury laws which have ever been enacted have been able to accomplish but little in enabling the borrower to secure loans at a less rate than that prescribed by competition. The reason for this is plain on consideration. The total supply of accumulated wealth of the whole civilized world is engaged in this competition, and the millions of wealth which are added every day are new contestants in the market. Competition in other products is held in local bounds by the cost of shipment over long distances; but wealth in the form of value can be transferred quickly and easily to any part of the civilized world where a market awaits it. Every person who earns money or owns property is a potential competitor, in that he can be made to lend his capital for great enough inducements. Under the pressure of this competition, the price for the use of capital--the rate of interest--has steadily fallen; and the enormous production of wealth of which our industrial resources are now capable is such that the fall is certain to continue, and a very few years will see loans at 2 per cent. as common as those at 4 per cent. are to-day. Combination to restrict competition among those who loan capital for investment is an utter impossibility. The number of people with money to loan, or with property on which they can raise money for that purpose, if they wish, is too large a proportion of the population to be ever brought into a combination to restrict competition. The stringency which sometimes occurs in the money market need not be cited as a contradiction of this statement. That is a matter which has only to do with the currency. The broad fact, and it is a most important one, is that capital, a necessary agent of production, can never be monopolized.

X.

THE THEORY OF UNIVERSAL COMPETITION.

We have now examined all the important occupations in which men engage for the purpose of gain; and we have found that while certain large classes of men still have the returns for their industry fixed by the laws of competition, other large and important classes have been able to check and limit competition, so that their returns from their work are constantly increased; while others still, are in possession of certain agents, so necessary to the community and so rare, that a price can be exacted for their use greatly in excess of the original cost to their owners. Some of the effects of this state of affairs it is easy to perceive. We have, indeed, pointed out for each monopoly described some of the especial abuses to which it gives rise; and it is plain enough that the general tendency is, first, to greatly enrich the possessors of the strongest monopolies at the expense of all other men; second, to give a certain degree of advantage to the possessors of minor monopolies,--as, for instance, monopolies in articles which are luxuries, and can easily be dispensed with; and third, to seriously injure all those engaged in occupations in which the price of the product is still fixed by competition.

Every one will agree that this is an evil state of affairs. It is not just that my neighbor, who owns a mine or a railroad, should ask me what he pleases for coal, or for carriage of my produce to market; while I, being a farmer, must sell the products of my labor at a price determined by competition with the products of ten thousand other farms. No one can deny at this day that it is contrary to the principles of justice to give to the men in any one occupation or calling an advantage over those in any other, except in just the degree that one occupation is more beneficial to the world than another. The question then arises, how may we best remedy this state of affairs? Shall our panacea be to do away with all monopolies, and put every industry back upon the competitive system? If so, by what means are we to apply this remedy? Or shall we go to the other extreme and adopt the antipodal doctrine to the foregoing, that competition is an evil which ought to be done away with; and then proceed to abolish competition in every trade and occupation where it still exists, if we can find any possible means of accomplishing such a task.

The investigation we have already pursued gives us no answer to these questions. We have thus far studied facts, and made little attempt to deduce from them general truths. We are now informed as to the widespread growth of monopoly; and we have paid some attention to the injustice and wrong to which it gives rise, in order that we may understand the urgent necessity for finding the right remedies, and finding them at once. Our study is henceforth to be devoted to this end. How shall we go about it? In the first place, it is evident that we might make a far wider and more detailed investigation of existing monopolies, and still be no nearer our desired end. We might study the facts concerning each especial railroad monopoly in the country, for instance, without reaching any valuable conclusion with regard to the proper method of restricting railroad monopolies in general. But if we were to take the monopoly exercised by a single railroad company, and study the principles on which it is founded and the laws by which it is governed, we might then be able to state something of value in reference to proper methods for its control. Evidently, then, principles rather than facts are to be the chief subjects of our future discussion, although, of course, we can only discover these principles by investigating the facts already found, together with others which may come to our notice.

Our very first and most obvious generalization from the facts which we have studied is, that in all the monopolies we have considered, the inherent principle is the same, and the effect on the community is of the same sort. Therefore, instead of hunting for separate remedies for railroad monopolies and trusts and labor monopolies, we will see what the general problem of monopoly is, and what is the general nature of the remedy that should be applied; the details applicable to each case will, of course, be different; but the underlying principle must be the same.

But if we examine our problem a little more closely we see that the word monopoly seems to be only a negative, expressing the fact that competition is absent. We will therefore direct our studies to competition itself, and will consider first its action as the basis of our social system.

In the most primitive condition of man which we can imagine, each person provided for his or her own need. The competition which then existed was not competition, in the sense which we use the word in this volume, but was a struggle for existence and a gratification of the baser desires, of the same sort as that which now prevails in the brute creation, resulting in a "survival of the fittest." With the introduction of the family relation, the principle of the "division of labor" was utilized, the female doing the hard and menial work, while the male devoted himself to hunting and fishing, or subsisting on the results of his helpmate's industry. As men's wants increased and they became more industrious in supplying them, this division of labor was extended. The man most skilful in fishing neglected the use of the bow and spear, and his surplus of fish he exchanged with his neighbor for the fruit of the chase. The very same principle applied to different tribes brought about the first commerce. A pastoral tribe, with large flocks and herds, exchanged their surplus products with less civilized tribes who continued to live by the chase, or with a more civilized people who had begun to till the soil.

It is plain that these were first steps in civilization. Man, so long as he supplies only such of his wants as he can supply with the labor of his unaided hands, must remain in a half-fed, half-clothed, and untaught condition, because his strength and skill, when diverted in the many directions which his wants require, are not enough to enable him, even when he spends all his time at work, to supply himself with more than the barest necessaries of life. It would be interesting to trace the development of this principle of action through its various stages down to the present time, when we see men everywhere working at various trades and occupations, and always to supply some want of their fellow-men. Every person in the community is absolutely dependent upon a multitude of others, most of whom he knows nothing of, for the supply of almost all his wants. Human society is thus growing more and more interwoven and interdependent. The motto of the Knights of Labor is a true one, apart from the altruism involved in it. "An injury to one is the concern of all," because the mass of humanity is connected and woven together by such strong ties of self-interest, as well as fraternity, that a calamity to any class or country is felt in some degree throughout the civilized world. This is vastly more true now than it was a half-century ago. Under such conditions as existed then, the doctrine of laissez-faire, that the government should confine itself to the prevention of violence and crime and the maintenance of national honor and integrity, letting alone the industries of the country to develop and operate according to natural laws, was not liable to do harm. But the conditions now are wholly changed. The interdependence of the community involves a moral inter-responsibility, and the time has come when we must recognize this by making it a legal responsibility as well.

We are now ready to consider in detail this inter-relationship of society, and to examine the natural laws which govern it. We have already stated the fact that, broadly speaking, each man is engaged in supplying the wants of his fellow men, because in that way better than in any other he can supply his own wants. We shall find this an easy matter to understand if we conceive that every man puts the products of his labor, of whatever sort it be, into a common public stock (offers it for sale), and takes out of this common stock (buys) the various articles which he wants. He does the first simply that he may do the second, not because he desires to benefit his fellow-men. The money which he receives (as we do not propose to consider here any questions regarding the currency) we may regard as simply a certificate that he has done a certain amount of work for the world, the measure of which is the number of dollars he receives; and on presentation of that certificate, he can obtain other articles which he desires.

We have next to consider the fact that there is a great variation in the amount which a man can take out from this common stock. One man is able to provide himself from the common stock with a host of luxuries, while another may only take out a scant supply of the barest necessaries of life. If this distribution operated with perfect equity, a man would be permitted to take out of this common stock exactly in proportion to the benefit which the world at large received from that which he put in. No human judgment, however, is competent to fix, with even an approach to precision, the relative actual benefit which each member of society renders to his fellow-men as a whole. But our social system effects that for us better than it could be fixed by any arbitrary human judgment. This it does by a law known as the law of supply and demand. Instead of the actual benefit, this law takes what people choose to consider as benefit, which is the granting of their desires, whether they desire things hurtful or beneficial. It is these desires for things which others can produce which constitute demand. It is to be borne in mind that this is a broad term, and includes not only desires for food, clothing, and actual things, but for service of every sort, in short, demand is the desire for any thing whatever for which people are willing to pay money. But when there is this demand-- this willingness to pay money for any article--people begin at once to supply it, because the money they receive allows them to take goods which they wish from the common stock. Evidently, if there is an unlimited supply of any thing, people will not pay money for it. People will not pay money for fresh air to breathe when they are out-of-doors, and the supply is unlimited; but when indoors, the supply may be limited, and they will spend money to have ventilators and air-pipes built to supply them with fresh air. Or take the contrary case: The supply of some commodity, say flour, falls very short. Evidently less flour must be used by the world than was used in the years of a more plentiful wheat harvest. But no one will wish to be the one to go without, and most people will pay a little more rather than do so. Therefore the price rises.

The competition which we have chiefly considered is the rivalry which exists between the men who supply the same sort of goods; but there is a rivalry among buyers as well. Speaking generally, every buyer is trying to purchase for as little as possible, and every seller is trying to dispose of his goods or services to the world for as much as possible, which each has a perfect right to do.

We have already seen that prices vary with the relative proportion between supply and demand, rising as demand rises or supply fails, and falling as supply increases or demand falls off. But to complete the wonderful perfection of the mechanism, the reciprocal relation is introduced, so that supply and demand vary with price. If the price rises, fewer people can afford to buy and more will be anxious to sell; while if the price falls, more people will wish to buy and fewer people will be willing to sell.

We can now easily see why some men are able to take out from the world's common stock of product so large an amount, while most men can take but a meagre allowance. By the law of supply and demand the price is far higher for the service which one man renders to the world than another. Let us take the operation of a large machine shop, for instance. Only one superintendent is needed, and he should be a man who has devoted much time to mastering all the details of the business, and is experienced and competent to so govern the work that a large product will be turned out at a small expense. There is a demand in the country, let us say, for 5,000 such men; but out of the 5,000 who are filling such places, there are perhaps 50 who seem almost faultless in their skill and industry, there are 500 who are with one or two exceptional faults, almost equally efficient, there are 3,000 who are fairly good men, and the rest may be classed as those who hold their positions because better men for the place cannot be had. So with the skilled machinists, the relation of supply and demand is such that the price of their labor is kept up to perhaps $4.00 per day. But of common laborers the supply is so related to demand that the price of their work is very low. Thus the three classes take very unequal amounts from the common stock. The superintendent, perhaps, is able to take five thousand dollars' worth of goods each year. The skilled workman can spend perhaps one thousand five hundred dollars, while the laborer can spend but five or six hundred dollars. Thus the men who secure the greatest amount of wealth in return for their services to the world, secure it because people are willing to pay it rather than pay less for men of less ability. This is not the same as rewarding a man according to the actual benefit which he does to the community, but it is an approach to it; and it seems to be as close an approach as is possible by human methods.

This social system is not the creation of any man or set of men, but has grown of itself out of the tendency among men to secure the things they wish for with the least exertion. And its theoretical working is marvellously perfect. Any thing which men desire sufficiently to exert themselves to secure it, can be bought with a small part of the time and labor, measured in money, which would be required if each made it for himself. Not only this, but the aim of every man is to do the greatest service to the world and best meet its desires, thus securing in return the greatest rewards for himself. Rivalry among purchasers constantly tends to increase the rewards of the producers, while competition among the latter tends toward the furnishing of a better article at a smaller price. These two forces hold each other in stable equilibrium, for a variation tends always to bring things back to their normal condition.

Let us look more closely at the theory of the competition among producers. We see that, speaking broadly, all occupations are competing with each other. If changes in the supply or demand raise the rewards in any calling, men will leave other work to engage in it. Men by the pressure of competition are forced to seek out the easiest and most direct methods, and to learn how to secure the greatest results with the least expenditure of labor and material.

It is this principle which lies at the very root of our industrial development. Men have so striven to meet each other's competition and outstrip each other in the production of superior goods at low prices, that the cost of the staple articles of consumption, measuring by the labor required to produce them now and the labor required by the clumsy tools and hand work of a century ago, is from a tenth to a hundredth of the cost in those days. It must be remembered, too, that this system of competition is in accordance with the sense of inalienable personal rights which is implanted in the breast of every man. The work of my hands and brain are my own. In disposing of it for a price, I have a right which none may deny to obtain such a sum as I can induce any one to pay me. If I choose to sell it for less than my neighbor, it is my right. In short, the open market is open to all; and every man has a right to sell there his labor, his skill, or his goods, of whatever sort he can produce, at such a price as he can obtain. The same is true of the buyer. I have a right to go into the open market and secure such goods as any one wishes to sell me at the lowest price for which he will part with them. A curious illustration of this sense of personal right is the custom duties on imported goods. It is an evidence of this inherent feeling of a natural right that both public opinion and the law hold that it is a much less serious crime to smuggle than to steal. There are a dozen people who would smuggle, if tempted to do so, to one who would steal. Another illustration is the opposition shown to sumptuary laws on the same grounds.

It is to be said that the fact that competition lies at the foundation of our industrial civilization, tersely expressed in the saying, "Competition is the life of trade," has long been known, and, to a certain extent, appreciated. The common law, based on the decisions of men most eminent for wise insight and sound judgment, has always held that combinations to restrict competition and establish a monopoly were contrary to public policy, and the protection of the law has invariably been refused, whether they were combinations of labor or of capitalized industries. The establishment of labor combinations, indeed, was long a criminal offence, as we have pointed out more fully in the chapter devoted to that subject. It must be said, too, that the principle has come to be generally, though rather blindly, understood by the masses of men. It is recognized, though perhaps not very clearly, that competition lowers the prices of goods, and that this benefits every consumer. Let a proposition to build a competing railroad line, or a competing electric-light plant be submitted to popular approval, and, under the impression that they are benefiting themselves, hard-working men will cheerfully assume heavy burdens of taxation to aid the new enterprise. So blind and unreasoning indeed, is this popular abiding faith in the merits of competition, that it has been responsible for some of the greatest wastes of wealth in unproductive enterprises that have ever been known.

We have now examined the theory of universal competition as commonly accepted at the present day, and it is rightly considered a fundamental principle of society. It is the practice of most economic writers of the orthodox school to lay great stress on the importance of this fundamental principle, and enlarge upon its various manifestations. The many attempts to limit and destroy competition, which we have studied, they consider merely as abnormal manifestations which are opposed to law, and so not worth while considering very fully. But we have seen clearly to what extent the destruction of competition has gone on; and, with this knowledge, the question almost inevitably occurs to us: Is not this decay and death of competition, this attempt to suppress it under certain conditions, too wide and general a movement to be treated as merely a troublesome excrescence? Is it not likely that there are certain fixed laws regarding competition which determine its action and operation, and sometimes its death? If this be so, it is of the highest importance that we find and study these laws; and to that purpose we will devote the following chapter.

XI.

THE LAWS OF MODERN COMPETITION.

Thus far in our study, we have assumed that we knew what competition was. Now, however, as we are to study it scientifically, we are in need of an exact definition, that we may know just what the term includes. Prof. Sturtevant, in his "Economics," says: "Competition is that law of human nature by which every man who makes an exchange will seek to obtain as much as he can of the wealth of another for a given amount of his own wealth." Simmer this down to its essence, and we have simply: Competition is selfishness. To the other evident faults of the definition we need not allude. It is a much more satisfactory definition which Webster's Dictionary gives us, for it includes the idea that competition necessitates two or more parties to exercise it: "Competition is the act of seeking the same object that another is seeking." But this is too broad a definition for our purpose. It takes in competitions for fame, social standing, etc., with which we have nothing to do.

Failing to find a satisfactory definition, let us make one, as follows: Competition is that force of rivalry between buyers or between sellers which tends to make the former give a greater price for the commodity they wish to secure, and tends to make the latter offer better commodities for a less price.

That competition is a force, even in the popular estimation, is evidenced by such common expressions as "the pressure of competition," "a strong competition," and indeed, "the force of competition." But these very expressions show us as well, what we have already found to be true in the preceding chapters, that it is not a constant force but a variable one. What, then, are the laws of its variation?

Let us see what we can learn by a study of three typical examples of the force of competition. Let us take first the business of growing corn. There are perhaps three million farmers in the United States engaged in producing corn, and each one of these competes with all the others. Is this doubted? We have defined competition as a rivalry that tends to make the sellers offer better goods for a less price. Now at first sight it may seem that there is no rivalry at all. Neighboring farmers work together in all harmony; and no man thinks that because his neighbors have raised a large crop of corn, he is in any way injured. And yet this tendency to give better goods and lower prices exists and is plainly felt. Suppose a new and superior variety of corn were introduced, which buyers preferred. Some farmers would at once begin to raise it, so that they might be more sure of a market and perhaps of a better price, and other farmers would be obliged to follow suit to meet the competition. Again, consider that the supply and demand adjust themselves to each other through competition. For suppose, at the ruling price, the demand to be less than the supply; then to increase the demand, the price must fall; and the cause of the fall in price is simply that the farmers compete with each other for the market, and lower their prices in order to secure a sale for their crops. Note, however, that the rivalry in this case never becomes a personal one. Each farmer recognizes that an increased supply lessens the price for his goods; but his neighbor's extra acreage is such a drop in the bucket, that he never thinks of it as being really a rival of his own crop.

Take as a second example, the wholesale paper trade. Here are perhaps three hundred men, each knowing personally many of his competitors and probably hating some of them cordially. Each striving to secure for himself all the trade possible, and to gain, if he can, his rivals' customers. He sends out his salesmen with instructions to, "Sell goods! For the best prices you can get, but sell them, anyhow." These "drummers" are sharp, active business men, they might well be employed in directing some productive process; but they go out and spend their time in inducing customers by all the means in their power to buy their goods. They spend money in various "treats" to secure the good-fellowship of the man with whom it is desired to trade, and use his time as well as their own. Another item of expense is for advertising and for keeping the firm name prominently before the purchasing public. All these things cost money, as any wholesale merchant engaged in a business where there is sharp competition can testify. It may be thought that a firm which would have the courage to do away with all these expenses and give the money thus saved to their patrons in reduced prices and better goods, would be able to keep its trade and even gain over its competitors. But it is hardly so; most men are more likely to be wheedled into taking slightly inferior goods at a slightly greater price.

Another matter to be considered in this connection is the variation in price. In the case of the producers of corn, we saw that prices were practically uniform at any given place, being fixed by the ratio of supply and demand in the chief markets of the world. But in making sales of paper, the sharp, close-dealing buyer is generally able to secure a better price than a buyer not posted in regard to the condition of the paper trade.

As competition becomes more intense, its burdens become more heavy to carry. Perhaps two of the largest houses in the trade, who are able to force prices lowest, come to a sort of tacit understanding that their salesmen "will respect each others rights a little and not force prices down beyond all reason." It is plain that here the foundation is laid for the establishment of a monopoly. Yet the agreement certainly seems to be nothing more than these two firms have a right to make. Its result is seen, however, in a slight increase in the price their customers have to pay. Soon the tacit agreement becomes a formal one. Then other firms are taken in. The first seed has borne fruit. The combination grows larger and stronger. The number of producing units is growing less. Finally it includes practically all the paper manufacturers in the country. Whoever wants paper must buy of the combination, there is no other source of supply. Competition is dead.

If the combination is strong enough and is managed well enough, it may be permanent; and prices of paper will be regulated by other laws than the law of competition. But suppose that the number of paper makers is so great and that they are so widely scattered that the combination proves difficult to maintain;

local jealousies creep in, and charges are made of partiality on the part of the managers. The combination finally breaks up. Can we expect a perfect return to the old system of free competition? When men have once reaped the enormous returns that are yielded by the control of a monopoly, the ordinary profits of business seem tame and dull. There will surely be attempts to form the monopoly anew on a stronger and more permanent basis; and even if these attempts do succeed in producing only short-lived monopolies, the effect will be to keep the whole trade and all dependent upon it in a state of disquiet and uncertainty. Prices will swing up and down very suddenly between wide limits; and it is everywhere recognized that stability in price is a most important element in inducing general prosperity. A perusal of the trade journals for the years 1887 and 1888 will convince one of the truth that when a combination is once formed, its members are loth to try competition again. A considerable number of combinations which were formed in 1887 were soon broken up, often from the strength of old feuds and jealousies. But in almost every case they have been formed anew on a stronger basis after a short experience of competition.

This matter of the variation in price is a very important one, and it has an important influence in checking business prosperity. Men are far less apt to engage in an enterprise, if they cannot calculate closely on prices and profits. But the main point, after all, is the waste which is due to competition. It is for the interest of the public at large that the papermakers should devote all the energies which they give to their business to making the best quality of each grade of paper with the least possible waste of labor and material.

Take for a third example two railway lines doing business between the same points. We have fully pointed out the practical working of this sort of competition in the chapter devoted to railways. It is plain that the general effect is a fluctuation of rates between wide limits, an enormous waste of capital and labor, and ultimately, the permanent death of competition by the consolidation of the two lines.

In comparing now the above three cases, the most noticeable difference in the conditions is in the number of competing units. There were in the first example three million competitors; in the second, three hundred; and in the last, but two.

The first difference in the competition which existed is in intensity. In the case of the producers of corn, competition was so mild that its very existence was doubted. In the case of the papermakers it was vastly more intense, so that it caused those engaged in it to take steps to restrict and finally abolish it. In the case of the railroads it was still more intense, so that it was not able to survive any length of time, but had to suffer either a temporary or permanent death very soon. Let us state, therefore, as the first law of competition, this: In any given industry the intensity of competition tends to vary inversely as the number of competing units.

We also saw that among the producers of corn there was virtually no waste of energy from competition. Among the paper makers there was a large waste. And in the case of the railroads, the whole capital invested in the rival railroad, as well as the expense of operating it, was probably a total waste. Let us state, then, for a second law of competition: In any given industry the waste due to competition tends to vary directly as the intensity. As an additional example to prove the truth of these laws, take the competition which exists between buyers. In the case of ordinary retail trade the number of buyers is very great, and the competition between them is so moderate that we hardly remember that it exists. It is difficult to see how there could be any waste from this competition among buyers, at least of any amount. Expressed in the language of the laws we have found: The number of competing units is so great that competition is neither intense nor wasteful.

From these two laws and a study of the examples we have given, it is easy to deduce a third. We have seen that when competition became very wasteful, monopoly arose; indeed, we have noted the working of this law all through our investigation. The principal cause assigned for the formation of the linseed-oil trust was the waste which intense competition had caused. The third law is, then: In any given industry the tendency toward the death of competition (monopoly) varies directly with the waste due to competition.

We might now combine these three laws to deduce the fourth law, which is: In any given industry the tendency toward the death of competition (monopoly) varies inversely with the number of competing units. But this law is also proved independently. Look back over all the monopolies we have studied, and it will be seen that one of the most important conditions of their success was the small number of competitors. Fifty men could be brought together and organized, and made to bury their feuds and rivalries, when with a thousand the combination would have been impossible. We have seen, in the case of the farmers, how their great number alone has prevented them from forming combinations to restrict the competition among themselves.

It should be said that these laws, like all other laws of economics, are not to be taken in a narrow mathematical sense. We cannot study causes and effects dependent on the caprice of men's desires and wills with the minute exactness with which we solve numerical problems. Taken in the broad sense, however, the study we have made in the preceding chapters is sufficient proof of their truth.

The common expressions of trade afford still further evidence. We often hear the expression: "A healthy competition." But the very existence of the phrase implies that there may be an unhealthy competition, and if so, what is it? Is it not that competition whose intensity is so great that it causes a large waste of capital and labor in work other than production; whose intensity is so great that, like an animal or a machine working under too great a load, it labors intermittently,--now acting with great intensity and forcing prices far below their normal plane, now pausing in a reaction, when a temporary combination is formed, and allowing prices to spring back as far above the point indicated by the relation of supply and demand; and finally reaching the natural end for unhealthiness--death. In fact, a recent economic writer declares that especially intense competition should be called war, as, indeed, it frequently is called, rather than competition.

Looking about us for other causes of variation in the intensity of competition we discover a fifth law: The intensity of competition tends to vary directly in proportion to the amount of capital required for the operation of each competing unit, especially when the interest on the capital invested forms a large proportion of the cost of production. Take, for example, the case of a railway line. All the capital invested in it is wasted unless the road is in operation. Hence it will be better to operate the road, so long as receipts are any thing more than the expense of operation, than to abandon it. An enterprise in which no capital is invested will cease operations when receipts do not exceed its expenditure and there is no prospect of betterment. But in the total expense of operating a railroad, a large item is the interest on the capital invested, which is as truly a part of the total cost of carrying the traffic as is the daily labor expended in keeping the road in good repair. (In railway bookkeeping only an arbitrary line can ever be drawn between capital account and operating expenses.) Now, in order to pay operating expenses and fixed charges, railways must secure traffic. We suppose that they are doing this by competition, and that they have not yet combined to form a monopoly. Let us suppose that this competition cuts down receipts to a point where they are just sufficient to pay the whole cost of carriage. In an enterprise in which no capital was invested some of the competitors would be sure to fall out when profits disappeared; but here there is no such chance of relief; and though the competition keeps on until the receipts are only enough to pay the operating expenses, still the road is not abandoned because then the capital invested, in it would be a complete loss. Changes in productive processes often lessen the demand for a line of goods; but the owners of the capital invested in factories and machines for making these goods may often cause them to be continued in operation at a loss rather than lose all that they have invested, and because they hope for better days and a renewal of the demand.

For the sixth law of competition we have: In any given industry the tendency toward the death of competition (monopoly) varies directly with the amount of capital required for each competing unit. This law is proven in part by the preceding laws; for when a large capital is required for each competing unit, the number of competitors will be small and the tendency toward monopoly will be strong; but it may also be proven independently. Business men, before they form a combination, are certain to ask whether new competitors are likely to enter the field against the combination. Now, as we have seen in very many cases in the preceding chapters, when there is a great amount of capital required, new competitors will be very unlikely to enter the field. If there is but little capital required, they will be very apt to do so, being tempted by the prospect of large profits at the monopoly's prices. But they know that the combination will concentrate its strength to fight them in every way; and if they must invest a great deal of money in buildings, plant, etc., to start operations, they will be apt to think twice before they take the field against the combination.

The seventh law of competition is: In any given industry in which natural agents are necessary, the tendency toward the inequality of competition (monopoly) tends to vary directly with the scarcity of available like natural agents.

The influence of limited natural agents in promoting the growth of monopolies is a matter of the greatest importance. That the law is true, is evident upon slight investigation. For if some especial gift of Nature is a necessity to any industry, and those who are engaged in that industry can secure all the available gifts of Nature of that sort, there is no opportunity for new competitors to enter the field.

It is to be noted that in this seventh law we have used in apposition with the term monopoly, the term "inequality of competition" instead of "death of competition," as in the preceding laws. We are now in need of a definition of the term monopoly. Webster defines it as "the sole control over the sale of any line of goods"; Prof. Newcomb says "a monopoly is the ownership or command by one or a limited number of persons of some requisite of production which is not solely a product of human labor"; Sturtevant says "a monopoly is such a control of the supply of any desirable object as will enable the holder to determine its price without appeal to competition." To the first definition we object that it is both narrow and indefinite. The second seems to omit such important classes of monopolies as the combinations to limit competition; and Sturtevant's definition is unscientific in this: Hardly any monopoly exists whose holders can without limit determine the price of its product. If the price continues to rise, competition in some form will appear. Take, for example, the business of transporting goods from New York to San Francisco; if all the railway lines combine to form a monopoly, the competition of ocean steamers via Panama would eventually stop the rise in rates, if no other outside competition stopped it before. The owners of a rich mine have a real monopoly, though they cannot raise the price above a certain point without being undersold by the owners of poorer mines or those more remote from market. Consideration of these facts lead us to construct the following definition: A monopoly in any industry consists in the control of some advantage over existing or possible competitors by which greater profits can be secured than these competitors can make. For the law of monopolies we have: The degree of a monopoly depends upon the amount of advantage which is held over existing or possible competitors. When the advantage of the monopoly is so great that no other competitor will try to do business in competition with it, we may rightly say that competition is dead. The great share of the monopolies which are based on this seventh law of competition, those due to the control of natural agents, only restrict competition by the attainment of an advantage over their competitors, and do not destroy it.

The principal natural agents which are necessary to production, and whose supply may be so limited to cause an appreciable monopoly, are: (1) Land for agricultural purposes; (2) land for purposes of manufacture or commerce; (3) transportation routes, such as mountain passes, room for railway tracks in a city street, or for gas-and water-pipes beneath its surface; (4) natural deposits of minerals and metals; (5) sources of water supply or water power. (The latter is unimportant now compared with a score of years ago, because of the lessened cost of its competitor, steam.)

Let us be especially careful not to confound this seventh law of competition with a certain doctrine which is now receiving more and more credence, which is, in brief, that the private ownership of the gifts of Nature used in production should be abolished. The grounds in opposition to this doctrine we will discuss in a later chapter. The law we have stated says nothing of the right or wrong of the private ownership of the gifts of Nature. What it does say is, that when any of these are limited in amount, those who control them are given an advantage over other would-be competitors, which constitutes a monopoly.

In considering the natural agents enumerated above, we can easily see the truth of the law. Agricultural lands, the most important of natural agents, are in this country so abundant that their rental is entirely fixed by competition. In England, where they are so much more limited in area, rent is fixed by custom. As regards land for purposes of manufacture or commerce, we have already pointed out the cases in which monopolies are prominent, as also for transportation routes. As regards mineral wealth, deposits of iron are so numerous and widespread that no monopoly has ever yet succeeded in controlling competition in the manufacture of pig-iron to any great extent. But the rarer metals, like copper, tin, nickel, and others, are largely controlled by monopolies.

Now, while this seventh law says nothing as to the right or wrong, the expediency or inexpediency of the private ownership of natural wealth, it does follow from it that this private ownership generally constitutes a monopoly, as we have defined it. For of no class of natural agents is it true that their richness and availability are absolutely equal. Those competitors who have the richest and best natural resources to work with have an advantage over their competitors which is essentially a monopoly. Thus the owners of fertile lands near a large city have an advantage over the owners of less fertile lands far removed from markets, which is of a monopolistic nature. If any one doubts this, let him say how this case is logically different from that of the ownership of a mine of native copper so near to New York City that the cost of laying it down in the market there will be half what it is from any existing mine; or, for a second case, take the New York Central railway, which has the control of such a valuable pathway between the Mississippi Valley and the Atlantic seaboard that it has an advantage over all competitors in the business of transportation between those points.

We have now to turn our attention to other variations in competition besides the variation in intensity. We need to distinguish the different species of competition. That competition which is in daily operation in most branches of industry we may call actual competition. That competition which would spring up in any industry in case an increase in profits called it out, we may call potential competition. The third class is instanced in the letting to the highest bidder a franchise for city water or gas-works, or street-car lines. Here competition acts at a single time to fix the price for perhaps twenty years. We may call this, for want of a better name, franchise competition. It possesses the evident advantage that it avoids both the waste of competition and the fluctuation of prices. It has the disadvantage that, unless the owners of the franchise are held strictly to their contract, quality is apt to be sacrificed; also that if the purchase is for a term of years, cheapening in processes may result in undue profits to the franchise holders. The discussion of this matter, however, does not properly belong to this chapter.

Arranging in their logical order the laws of competition which we have found, we have the following diagram:

In any given industry the tendency toward monopoly increases:

(1.) As the waste due to competition increases.

The waste of competition increases in proportion to its intensity.

(1.) The intensity of competition increases as the number of competing units decreases.

(2.) The intensity of competition increases with the amount of capital required for each competing unit.

(2.) As the number of competing units decreases.

(3.) As the amount of capital required for each competing unit increases.

(4.) As the number of available natural agents decreases.

The preceding diagram sets plainly before us the three great salient causes from which have grown the long list of monopolies under which our civilization labors. First, the supply of natural agents of which new competitors in any industry may avail themselves has been largely exhausted, or has been gathered up by existing monopolies to render their position more secure; the world has not the natural resources to develop that she had a century ago. Second, the concentration of all the productive industries, except agriculture, into great establishments, while it has enormously lessened the cost of production, has so reduced the number of competing units that a monopoly is the inevitable final result. Last, the enormous capital required for the establishment and maintenance of new competing units tends to fortify the monopoly in its position and render the escape of the public from its grasp practically impossible. These terse statements contain exactly the kernel of potent truth for which we are seeking; MONOPOLIES OF EVERY SORT ARE AN INEVITABLE RESULT FROM CERTAIN CONDITIONS OF MODERN CIVILIZATION.

The vital importance of this truth cannot be over-estimated. For so long as we refuse to recognize it, so long as we attempt to stop the present evils of monopoly by trying to add a feeble one to the number of competing units, or by trying to legislate against special monopolies, we are only building a temporary dam to shut out a flood which can only be controlled at the fountain head.

The facts of history testify to the truth of this law. Monopolies were never so abundant as to-day, never so powerful, never so threatening; and with unimportant exceptions they have all sprung up with our modern industrial development. The last fifteen years have seen a greater industrial advancement than did the thirty preceding, but they have also witnessed a more than proportionate growth of monopolies. How worse than foolish, then, is the short-sightedness that ascribes monopolies to the personal wickedness of the men who form them. It is as foolish to decry the wickedness of trust makers as it is to curse the schemes of labor monopolists. Each is working unconsciously in obedience to a natural law; and the only reason that almost every man is not engaged in forming or maintaining a similar monopoly is that he is not placed in similar circumstances. Away, then, with the pessimism which declares that the prevalence of monopolies evidences the decay of the nobler aspirations of humanity. The monopolies of to-day are a natural outgrowth of the laws of modern competition, and they are as actually a result of the application of steam, electricity, and machinery to the service of man, as are our factories and railways. Great evils though they may have become, there is naught of evil omen in them to make us fear for the ultimate welfare of our liberties.

To the practical mind, however, the question at once occurs, what light have we gained toward the proper method of counteracting this evil? Can it be true that the conditions of modern civilization necessitates our subjection to monopolies, and that all our vaunted progress in the arts of peace only brings us nearer to an inevitable and deplorable end, in which a few holders of the strongest monopolies shall ride rough shod over the industrial liberties of the vast mass of humanity? Were this true, perhaps we had better take a step backward; relinquish the factory for the workshop, the railway for the stage-coach. "Better it is to be of an humble spirit with the lowly, than to divide spoil with the proud." But the law we have found commits us to no such fate. We cannot, indeed, abolish the causes of monopolies. We cannot create new gifts of Nature, and it would be nonsense to attempt to bring about an increase in the number of competing units and a decrease in the capitalization of each by exchanging our factories and works of to-day for the workshops of our grandfathers. But while monopolies are inevitable, our subjection to them is not inevitable; and when the public once comes to fully understand that the remedy for the evils of monopoly is not abolition, but control, we shall have taken a great step toward the settlement of our existing social evils. To discuss the details of the remedy, so far as it can be done in a volume of this sort, belongs properly to a later chapter. Before undertaking it, however, it seems well to devote some further attention to the evils which the attempt to abolish monopolies and adhere to the ideal system of universal competition has brought upon us, and to make, also, some further study of the general evils due to monopoly.

XII.

THE EVILS DUE TO MONOPOLY AND INTENSE COMPETITION.

It is a strange thing when we come to analyze the various social evils which demand our attention, and which every true man longs to cure, to find how great a proportion can be traced back to the one great evil of faulty competition. As a preliminary to a survey of these evils, in order that we may understand the necessity that all good men and true should exert themselves in applying the remedy, let us see just what conditions of our industrial society we should seek to work toward. What is the theoretical perfection of human industry?

Probably all thinking men, whatever their belief and practice, will acquiesce in the proposition that the end we should aim to secure is "the largest good to the greatest number." As we are discussing here only economic questions, this means that the end to be sought is that the largest number of people should have secured to them the greatest possible amount of the necessaries and comforts of life; or, more simply, that the total of human happiness to be derived from the world's production of wealth should be the greatest possible. Now for our present purpose we may assume that since all men desire wealth, the greater its production, the greater will be the number of human desires gratified. From this it follows that our social organization should be such as to increase to the greatest possible degree the world's stock of wealth.

There is no easier or safer way of studying questions of economics than to consider the community as a unit, and see what is for the interest of the people as a whole; what conduces most to the "common wealth"; and if we do this, whenever the question concerns production alone, the task is simple, because the interests of the people as a whole are judged in the same way as the interests of a single person. Whatever tends to increase the total amount of wealth in the world, therefore, benefits the community as a whole; and whatever diminishes the supply is an injury. All work of every sort which tends to aid in the economical production of wealth and its transfer to the consumer is a benefit to the community; and any thing which destroys wealth, lessens its production, or hinders men from exerting themselves to produce it, is an economic injury.

What, then, are we to say of the condition known as over-production? Is it not a fact that some lines of industry are so overdone that the production is far in excess of the demand, and is not this an evil rather than a benefit? Do not periods of business depression occur when all industries stagnate for want of a market for their goods? The true answer to this question is: Over-production is not a fault of production, but of distribution. It is true that, in special industries, a surplus of production sometimes occurs, due to over-stimulation, or too rapid growth; but over-production as commonly spoken of, refers to a general state of trade, in which demand for all sorts of goods seems to fall far below the market supply. But this lack of demand is not due to lack of desire. The desires of men are always in excess of their abilities to supply them; it follows, therefore, that the condition known as over-production consists in a lack of ability to purchase goods rather than in a lack of desire to purchase them. This lack of ability has evidently to do with the distribution of wealth rather than its production.

While it is easy to formulate laws to govern the theoretically perfect production of wealth, to whose justice all men will consent, we cannot go far in the details of the ideal distribution of wealth without reaching points upon which the views of different parties are diametrically opposed. Some foundation principles, however, let us state, believing that in their truth the great majority of men will concur.

In the chapter on the theory of competition we saw that, if we conceived the results of the labor of the whole community to be placed in a common storehouse and gave to each man the right to draw from it an amount just equal to the benefit derived from the goods which he had placed within it, the ideal of a perfect system of distribution of wealth would be realized. No human judgment, however, is, or ever can be, competent to measure the exact industrial benefits which each person confers upon the community at large. We must inevitably permit men to measure the result of their own work by securing for it such an amount of the results of others' work as they can induce them to give in exchange. But while we cannot measure exactly the benefit which each person confers, we can see cases in which the reward received is manifestly out of all proportion to the benefit conferred. Consider the fortunes which have been accumulated by some of our Midases of the present decade. It is quite certain that the benefits which Cornelius Vanderbilt, for instance, conferred on the community by his enterprise and business sagacity, by his work in opening new fields of industry, forming new channels for commerce, etc., were so valuable that he honestly earned the right to enjoy a large fortune. It is equally certain that a great part of his gains had nothing whatever to do with any benefit conferred upon the community, and that the fortune of $100,000,000 or so which he accumulated was an example of inequitable distribution of the products of the world's industry. Stating this in the form of a general principle, we should say: The amount of wealth which any man receives should bear some approximate relation to the benefit which he confers upon the world.

We have already stated that, by the law of supply and demand, the rewards of each worker are regulated in theory even more perfectly in accordance with our ideas of liberty than they could be on the basis of actual benefit conferred. For it is inconceivable that people would submit to pay for what was beneficial to them instead of what they desired. A man who prefers to purchase wines instead of books with his surplus money would think it a great injustice if he were prevented from doing as he preferred with his own. But so long as every one is at liberty to use his income in buying whatever he desires most, demand--the willingness to pay money for the gratification of the desire--will exist, and so long as demand exists it will be met by a supply, furnished by those who are desirous of money and what it will bring. It is inconceivable, then, that any juster arrangement than this law of supply and demand can ever be practicable for regulating the compensation of each individual. The man who can drive a locomotive will receive larger wages than the man who shovels the earth to form its pathway, because the supply of men competent to drive an engine is small in proportion to the number of men who are wanted for that work, while almost any man can shovel dirt. Let us state, then, for our second principle: The amount of wealth which any man receives should depend on the ratio between the demand which exists for his services and the supply of those able to render like service. Farther than these statements of the ideal principles governing the economical production and equitable distribution of wealth we need not go at present.

Let us turn now to examine the result of a violation of these principles in some of the crying evils of the present day which are wholly or in part due to the growth of monopoly and the waste of competition.

Every candid man will acknowledge that the enormous congestion of wealth in a few hands which exists to-day is a danger to be feared. We have had it constantly dinned in our ears that in this free land the ups and downs of fortune were such that the rich man of to-day was apt to be the beggar to-morrow; also that almost invariably a rich man's sons were reckless spendthrifts. These things, aided by the abolition of primogeniture and entails, it was said, were to prevent the growth of a moneyed aristocracy in this country. The propounders of this amiable theory never explained how the community received reparation for the destruction of wealth which the spendthrift sons were to carry on; but so long as the theory has failed to work in practice, that does not matter so much.

A few years ago it was a favorite occupation of newspaper paragraphers to estimate the Gould and Vanderbilt fortunes; but lately they seem to have given them up as beyond the limits of even their robust guessing abilities. Some idea of the latter's fortune may be gained, however, by realizing the fact that the Vanderbilt railway system now has a total extent of nearly 12,000 miles, the total value of which can hardly be less than one thousand millions of dollars. Probably not less than half of the securities of these companies are owned by the Vanderbilt family, and it is well known that their investments are by no means confined to railways. The important fact is, that this fortune grows so fast now that it is sure to increase; and will double itself every fifteen or twenty years, because all that its owners can spend is but a drop in the bucket toward using up their income. But this fortune, while the largest which is still under one name, is but one of many enormous ones. The names of Gould, Flagler, Astor, Rockefeller, Stanford, Huntington, and a host of others follow close after the Vanderbilts. In the days of our grandfathers, millionaires were no more plentiful than hundred-millionaires are to-day.

We have next to show the present and prospective evils which result from this congestion of wealth. The first and most obvious one is its injury to the remainder of the people of the country, by the diversion from them of wealth which they have rightfully earned and which they would receive were it not for the tax of monopoly. It is obvious that a certain amount of wealth is annually produced by the industry of the country from which the whole wants of the country must be supplied. This amount may be greater, indeed, when a Gould or a Flagler or a Crocker directs the enterprise; but for the most part it is indisputable that the owners of these colossal fortunes have made them, not by any stimulus of the production of wealth by their owners, but by a diversion of the produced wealth in the general distribution from others' pockets to their own. In short, all other men are poorer that these many times millionaires may be richer. To show how these fortunes have in many cases been obtained, I cannot do better than to quote a writer not at all likely to err by undue severity to our millionaires, as he is himself the president of a railway system a thousand miles in extent:

The great majority of the phenomenal fortunes of the day are the result of what may be called lucky gambling.... Man is a gambling animal by nature, and modern methods have enormously developed both its facilities and its temptations and have opened large fields in which gambling is not held to be disreputable.

Under such stimulus is it wonderful that its growth has been phenomenal? Wall street is its head-quarters, and millions upon millions of dollars are accumulated there to meet the wants of the players. Railroad stocks are its favorite cards to bet upon, for their valuation is liable to constant fluctuation on account of weather, crops, new combinations, wars, strikes, deaths, and legislation. They can also be easily affected by personal manipulations.... Money makes money, and money in great masses has its attractive power increased. The aspect of phenomenal fortunes, therefore, is a social problem of some importance. Their manner of growth and their manner of use are to be observed, and what restrictions, if any, should be placed on their accumulation should be considered.[5]

[5] "Railway Practice." By E. P. Alexander, President Central Railroad and Banking Co. of Georgia.

The fact pointed out by General Alexander in the above quotation is one which is far too lightly appreciated. The evils of railway management by which the owners of the stocks and bonds of the company are victimized to enrich stock speculators are much too complex and numerous to be described here. The state of affairs can be briefly summed up, however, with the statement that our present system of conducting corporate enterprises results inevitably in the gravitation of their ownership into the hands of the holders of large fortunes. The railways of the country are an instance in point. Time was when the stocks and bonds of railways were owned by people of small means all over the country. But after many severe lessons in the shape of stocks wiped out, and bond interest scaled down, these small holders were taught the folly of investing their savings in business over which they had practically no control, and thus placing them at the mercy of irresponsible corporate officers. Broadly speaking, the railway property of the country is owned by men worth their millions; and the small holdings are being rapidly absorbed every day. But the case is not true of railways alone. Telegraph lines, telephone, and electric light plants, our mines, and to a large extent our factories, which were once held by private owners, are now controlled by corporations whose shares are quoted on the exchanges and are consequently subject to a forced variation, dictated according as "bull" or "bear" has the ascendancy. And when the ownership of a property is once brought into this channel, it is no longer a suitable investment for the man of small means. It is the prey of men who practically make bets as to what its future price will be, and manipulate the price, if possible, to win their bets. If it is ever again held for investment simply, it is when it is locked in the safe of some modern Croesus.

We have shown now the extent to which the congestion of wealth has gone. We have shown that other men are poorer that these men may be richer. We have explained that these great fortunes have been made, not by legitimate enterprise, but largely by "lucky gambling." And finally we have seen how the transfer of each enterprise to the control of stock speculators adds it eventually to some already overgrown fortune. The connection with the subject of the present volume is obvious. The cotton-seed oil mills of the South, once held by private owners, are now in the hands of a trust whose certificates are quoted on the stock-exchanges, and are held only by men of large capital, or by stock gamblers. This is a typical example of the change which is everywhere occurring. Private enterprise gives way to the stock company, and that in turn gives way to the trust. The salient fact, then, we may express in similar terms to those of our first law of competition, as follows: The congestion of wealth tends to increase inversely with the number of competing units.

The facts we have stated make it impossible for the greater monopolies to defend themselves, on the ground that their profits inure to the benefit of any great number of people. But this is not an innocuous state of affairs. It is one of serious injustice and evil. The workman who struggles hard to save a hundred dollars a year can receive only a paltry three dollars and a half of interest or less, if he deposits it in a saving-bank. But the capitalist who is clearing a hundred thousand a year may make twice or thrice that interest from his investments. In short, the charge is: That monopoly and intense competition, with the variation in price which they cause, have shut out the small capitalists of the country from the ownership of the most profitable sorts of property; and by confining them to other lines, have decreased their possible income from their investments.

A further evil resulting from the congestion of wealth is what is commonly spoken of as over-production. We are confronted of late years with the strange spectacle of factories and mills shut down for months at a time, of markets which, at various times, are glutted with every sort of commodity. All sorts of causes are given; all sorts of remedies are suggested and tried. Where is the true one? With the exception of a few special cases, the fault is not that there are no people who want the goods. Probably ninety-nine families out of every hundred would buy more if they had the money to buy with. In many cases the lack of money to buy with is due to the fact that the bread-winners are out of employment because of the glutted markets and idle mills. In this way the evil tends to perpetuate itself and grow worse. Now combine this fact with the fact that the holders of monopolies are in the receipt of incomes so great that, in many cases, they are quite unable to spend them. Also, that this income is largely locked up to wait the chance of profitable investment, or is used in speculation. Is it not obvious, now, that the reason why people cannot afford to purchase the goods, with which the storehouses are glutted, is that too large a proportion of profits has been diverted to swell fortunes already enormous? Have we not in this way accounted for a large amount, at least, of the over-production which is throwing out of employment thousands of workmen, rendering useless a vast amount of valuable capital, and affecting from time to time the business of the whole country with a veritable paralysis?

The facts bear out this theory. For, at many times when producers in every industry are complaining of dull times because people who buy have no money to spend, there is an abundance of money to be had for investment. Fortunately, the evil seen from this aspect must, to a certain extent, be but a temporary one, and will tend to work its own cure. For as the world's stock of invested wealth continues to grow, there is less opportunity for its profitable investment in improving undeveloped natural resources. The greater portion of our wealth we save and invest, the faster will the rate of interest tend downward. But, as this occurs, the operators of mills and mines have to pay less out of their receipts as interest on their borrowed capital, and can, therefore, pay more to their workmen.

There is another way in which monopoly works to cause over-production, with its attendant evils. Suppose a trust is formed in some manufacturing industry, where the working capacity is just equal to supplying the demand. The first work of the trust is to raise the prices perhaps 20, 30, or 40 per cent. Of course this causes a falling off in the demand, and the trust has to shut down some of its mills to ward off over-production. The true cause of over-production in this case is, that the prices are not in equilibrium with the relation between supply and demand. Let prices come down, and the demand will increase. The working of this special case gives us an idea of the way in which general over-production is caused. For it is well known that monopolies have raised the prices and reduced the consumption not of one, but of hundreds of articles. If the men who are made idle by the over-production in these industries flock into other occupations to secure work, they reduce wages there; so that, in any case, their purchasing power is reduced, and this tends to perpetuate and increase the evil. Of course it is not pretended to claim that all industrial depressions have been due to over-production, or the local congestion of the world's income. But that a large part of it may be justly laid to this cause, seems to be beyond question.

We have shown that the congestion of wealth is very largely due to the growth of monopoly, and we have discussed the more immediate evils that result from this congestion of wealth. But when we attempt to describe the evils and abuses which follow close after, as a result of the power which monopoly has placed in the hands of a few, we may well pause at the task. The whole array of perplexing social problems comes before us, and we realize more and more what a curse monopoly has become. The philanthropist tells us that poverty, and all the distresses that follow in its wake, are largely due to the fact that our workingmen under present conditions must live from hand to mouth, must rely on charity for aid in every emergency, and must, therefore, decrease in manliness and self-reliance and the ambition to better themselves, as the practical impossibility of success is comprehended.

Good men are lamenting because the Church has, to a great degree, lost its hold on the laboring classes, and are casting about on all sides for a remedy. Will they ever find one as long as the wage-worker carries in his bosom a rankling sense of injury done him? Injury which he feels that the Church is merely seeking to drug with charity instead of wishing to cure it with justice? There is great need that the Church, not alone by the sermons of its most enlightened thinkers, like Dr. Heber Newton, but by the daily practice of the rank and file of its membership, should recognize, as it never yet has done, the great principles of human fraternity, and move intelligently and earnestly to remedy the great evils that menace us.

Even the evil of intemperance can be traced back to a connection with monopoly. Who shall blame the tired laborer, if after a week with sixty hours of unremitting toil, he takes refuge from the dreariness and lassitude of physical exhaustion, the hopelessness of ambition-quenched life, and perhaps the discomforts and disquiet of the place he calls home, in a long draught of that which does, for the time, create in him an image of exhilaration, strength, self-respect, and manhood? It is but an image, indeed, and to all but the victim it is a caricature; but when a man cannot hope for the reality, to only imagine for a brief hour that he is indeed a king of men, and that care and woe and degradation are no longer his lot, is a refuge not to be despised.

There is indeed a class of philanthropists who say, with some truth, that the laboring classes as a whole have now more than they will spend for their own good, and declare that higher wages means merely more spent on sprees and debasing sports, of different sorts but universally harmful. On the other side, the wise philanthropists who are trying to help their fellow-men in that best of all ways, by teaching them to rely on themselves, testify that their efforts to make men independent are largely hampered because it is so extremely difficult for a workingman to live in any other way than from hand to mouth, especially in our large cities. The true solution seems to be that all these reforms must go hand in hand. We must teach men how to make nobler uses of their incomes and themselves, while we endeavor to bring about reforms that shall give them greater comforts and more leisure to use for either self-improvement or self-debasement.

Much more might be said of the indirect effects which result from the taxation which monopolies inflict upon the community for their own profit; but they are now so generally realized and understood that we can devote our time more profitably to the investigation of other evils.

Under the ideal system of competition which we studied in Chapter X., we found that all occupations were competing with each other; so that if, from any cause, one calling became especially profitable, men would flock to it and bring down the profits to a normal point. Monopolies have seriously interfered with this important and beneficent law. How often do we hear the complaint of the great difficulties that beset young men on their first entrance to business or industrial life in securing a situation. The monopolized industries shut out new competitors by every means in their power. The trade-unions limit the number of apprentices which shall be allowed to learn their trade each year. The result is, first, a most deplorable tendency to idleness on the part of young men just at the time when they should be most active; and, second, a still larger increase of men in the professions and non-monopolized callings, tending to still further increase the competition in those callings, where returns are already inferior to what they should be. Surely, we must begin to appreciate how vitally important to every person in the land is this matter of competition and monopoly.

The evils which we have thus far considered pertain to the distribution of wealth. Let us now turn our attention to the production of wealth. Our second law of competition stated that the waste due to competition varied directly as its intensity. We have frequently referred to this waste of competition; let us now inquire more fully concerning its amount and effect. In the first place, however, let us settle the question, once for all, that waste or destruction of wealth of any sort is an economic injury to the community. We have, indeed, already explained this in the first paragraphs of the chapter; but while all authorities on economics agree on this point, the general public is still seriously infected with the fallacy that waste, destruction, and unprofitable enterprises are beneficial because they furnish employment to labor. If this were merely a theory, we could afford to ignore it; but the trouble is that it is acted upon, and works untold evil and damage to the world. To take a typical case, people reason that damage done by flood or fire or storm is not a total loss because employment will be furnished to many in repairing and rebuilding after the devastation. They do not stop to reflect that so much wealth has been wiped out of the world, and that instead of the destruction furnishing so much additional employment, it has only changed the direction of the employment. For money nowadays is always spent, either directly, by its owners, or by some one to whom he lends it. And wherever money is spent it furnishes employment. Therefore, if the money which was used in repairing and rebuilding had not been required for that work, it would have been spent in some other direction and furnished employment to labor there. Understanding, then, that the economic interests of the community are best served when each one of its members exerts his energies with the greatest result and with the least waste in producing wealth, let us see to what extent intense competition and monopolies have violated this law.

In his interesting book entitled "Questions of the Day," Prof. Richard P. Ely, of Johns Hopkins University, refers to the building of two great railways with closely paralleled roads already in operation, the Nickel Plate, and the New York, West Shore and Buffalo, and says:

"It is estimated that the money wasted by these two single attempts at competition amounts to $200,000,000. Let the reader reflect for a moment what this means. It will be admitted that, taking city and country together, comfortable homes can be constructed for an average of $1,000 each. Two hundred thousand homes could be constructed for the sum wasted, and two hundred thousand homes means homes for one million people. I suppose it is a very moderate estimate to place the amount wasted in the construction of useless railroads at $1,000,000,000, which, on the basis of our previous calculations, would construct homes for five millions of people. But this is probably altogether too small an estimate of even the direct waste resulting from the application of a faulty political economy to practical life. When the indirect losses are added, the result is something astounding, for the expense of a needless number of trains and of what would otherwise be an excessively large permanent force of employees must be added. Of course, nothing much better than guesswork is possible, but I believe that the total loss would be sufficient to provide a greater portion of the people of the United States with homes."

But it seems quite possible to make a closer estimate of the wealth wasted by the construction of unneeded railways than the general one above. There are now, in round numbers, 158,000 miles of railway in the United States. The two lines named above have a total extent of nearly 1,000 miles; and while they are the most flagrant examples of paralleling in the country, there is no small number of other roads in various parts of the country which, except for their competition with roads already constructed, would never have been built. Considering the fact that the paralleling has been done in regions where the traffic was heaviest and where the cost of construction was greatest, it seems a conservative estimate to say that 5 per cent. of the capital invested in railways in the United States has been spent in paralleling existing roads. But the total capital invested in the railways of the United States is about $9,200,000,000, 5 per cent. of which is $460,000,000. It is also to be remembered that this 7,500 miles of needless road has to be maintained and operated at an average expense per mile per annum of $4,381, or a total annual cost of nearly $33,000,000. Taking Prof. Ely's estimate of $1,000 as the cost at which an average size family can be provided with a comfortable home, and we find that the cost of these unneeded railways would have provided 460,000 homes, sufficient to accommodate 2,300,000 people. Say that 3 per cent. of the cost of these homes is required annually to keep them in repair, then this could be furnished by the $33,000,000 now paid for the operating expenses of needless railways, and an annual margin of about $19,000,000 would be left, or enough to provide each year homes for nearly 100,000 more people in addition. Of course, this is merely a concrete example of what possible benefits we have been deprived by wasting our money in building needless railways.

As a matter of fact, the money we have spent on unprofitable railways, as well as those totally useless, has wrought us an amount of damage far in excess of their actual cost. It is generally agreed by financiers that the periods of industrial depression during the past score of years have been largely due to excessive railway building. For in a period of active railway construction, roads are built whose only excuse for existence is that they will encroach upon the territory of some rival. The capital invested fails to make a return. The loss of income which ensues decreases the purchasing power of the community; and this combines with the sudden loss of business confidence caused by the failure of the enterprise to bring about a general panic and crash which affects the whole community; and by checking enterprise and industry, damages the country ten times the amount of the original loss.

The waste of competition is by no means confined to railways. The Sugar Refiners' trust has raised the price of sugar and thus reduced its consumption so much that they have permanently closed several of their factories. Yet Claus Spreckels is now building a great refinery in Philadelphia, the output of which is to compete with the trust. All this capital invested in that which is not needed by the community is an injury to the public. The French Copper syndicate so raised the price of copper that it became profitable to work old mines of poor ore, which under ordinary circumstances could not be worked at all at a profit. Capital was expended in opening and refitting these mines, and in preparing them for working; while other mines, able to produce the metal at much less cost, were reducing their output because of their contract with the trust.

In various cities of the country, millions have been wasted in tearing up the streets to bury the unneeded mains of competing gas companies. The electric light competitors are stringing their wires over our heads and beneath our feet, and by covering the same district twice or three times, double and treble the attendant evils as well as the cost.

The waste due to intense competition in trade may be avoidable or unavoidable; but it is certainly of enormous magnitude, although the fact of its being a waste is still little appreciated.

The waste due to labor monopolies is much better understood. The strikes which paralyze industry and send want and distress in ever widening circles are universally recognized to be a waste of wealth whose annual amount is enormous. The cost to employers and workmen of the strikes in the State of New York in 1886 and 1887, was $8,507,449. Reckoning from this as a basis, it is probable that the total annual cash cost of strikes in the United States is twenty or twenty-five million dollars. The results of these strikes in decreasing the purchasing power of employ 閥 and thus causing overproduction, and in discouraging enterprise and increasing the cost of capital, serve to spread their effect throughout the whole industrial community and thus cause an actual loss and injury many times that borne by the parties directly engaged.

It is thus evident that the waste due to the intense competition which the concentration of productive enterprise has brought about in modern times is a matter of startling proportions. We are wasting and destroying wealth all the time sufficient to go a long way towards abolishing all the poverty in our midst; and the blame for this state of affairs we are now able to place where it belongs.

Surely with a full appreciation of these evils, every honest and patriotic man must be willing to use every endeavor to strike at the root of the evil. The public indeed is, and has long been, a unit in its opposition to monopoly; but in endeavoring to defeat monopoly it has taken just the course which could give no permanent gain. Cities have beggared themselves to aid competing railway lines only to see them consolidated eventually with the monopoly which it was expected to defeat. The multitude regard Claus Spreckels as a benefactor--and will till he forces the Sugar Trust to divide their 25 per cent. profits with him in return for the control of his refinery.

It is no benefit to us if in steering away from the Scylla of monopoly, we be wrecked on the Charybdis of wasteful competition. We have been trying for a score of years now to defeat monopolies by creating competition; but in spite of a universal public sentiment in favor of the reform, and notwithstanding the millions of wealth which we have poured out like water to accomplish this object, monopolies to-day are far more numerous and powerful than ever before. The people who are groaning under their burden of oppression are anxious for relief. The remedy they have so long and faithfully tried to apply has but made a bad matter worse; and it is small wonder that, despairing of other relief, they are adopting false and injurious plans for bettering themselves which serve merely to extend the monopoly policy into all industrial affairs.

We are threatened with a state of society in which most of the principal industries will be wholly given over to monopoly. Those in each occupation will band together to secure the greatest returns for themselves at the expense of all other men; while the few occupations which cannot thus combine in a monopoly--farming, and the different sorts of unskilled labor--will be filled to overflowing with those crowded out of other callings. Those who follow them will do so only because the monopolized occupations are closed to them. Thus will our farming population degenerate into a peasantry more miserable than that of Europe, and our laborers be ground down to a level lower than they have yet known. Is there a probability that such a state of affairs will come to pass? There might be if the public were not keenly alive to the curse of monopoly. But as it is, the greater danger is that through ignorance a wrong course may be adopted for the cure of our present evils, which will aggravate instead of curing them.

XIII.

AMELIORATING INFLUENCES.

If pure selfishness were the only motive influencing the masses of mankind, the evils which we have considered in the preceding chapter would be wholly unbearable. All men would be waging an industrial warfare with each other in their greed for gain, just as the barons of feudal times fought to satisfy their thirst for power and possessions; and as motive is the great force which determines character, we would be, as far as moral excellence is concerned, in the same category as the uncivilized savages.

Fortunately for the happiness of the race, there are important influences at work counteracting, modifying and ameliorating the social evils that threaten us. These influences are not cures for these evils, though they are so considered by very many people. But they are very important palliatives. They are certainly of inestimable value in the lack of real remedies; but it is better to consider them as palliatives merely; for necessary, as they are and always will be, to soften and relieve the ruggedness of human laws and human administration of law, in the present condition of humanity they cannot effect a cure of the evils which burden us.

The first of these palliatives has a purely selfish origin. It arises from the desire of the managers of every monopoly to make the greatest possible profit from its operations. Let us take, for example, a street railway monopoly which is at liberty to charge such rates of fare as it chooses and which has no competitors. If it fixes its fare at 10 cents, very many people will prefer to walk or take some other mode of conveyance, who, if the fare was at 5 cents, would patronize the road. Thus it may very likely happen that 5-cent fares will yield it the greatest net income. It is often said that it is competition which has brought our rates of railroad transportation down to their present low point. While this is largely true, it is also true that the tendency to foster the growth of traffic by making a low tariff has been a large factor in bringing rates down to a reasonable point. Another example of this principle's operation is in the case of monopolies protected by the patent laws. In this case the collection of only a moderate royalty will generally result in greater profits to the inventor than he would secure by exacting a large fee, because of the greatly increased sales in the former case.

It should not be understood, however, that this principle has its only application in cases similar to the two mentioned. There is hardly an industry, monopolized or competitive, into which it does not enter to effect important results. It is to be noted, however, that it is least effective where the demand for the monopolized article is least sensitive to a variation in price. This fact should be considered by those who are fond of arguing that this principle alone is always sufficient to prevent monopolies from doing much harm. While it is powerful in the case of such monopolies as we have mentioned, where the demand for the commodity furnished varies greatly with the price, in the case of the great copper trust or of the quinine trust or of any monopoly controlling the great staples of human consumption, it seems plain that it can have little effect. Nor do we need to base our proof that this principle is not a sufficient remedy upon this ground alone. Grant it to be true that a certain monopoly makes the greatest net profit when its rates or prices are at a certain point; then will it not be apt to set them slightly above that point, where they will give nearly the same profit with a considerable decrease in the volume of business transacted and in the corresponding labor and responsibility? And, again, the point where it makes the greatest net profit is considerably above the point where it is of the greatest possible benefit to the community at large. This latter end is attained when it uses its facilities to their full capacity for the benefit of the public. The rates should be fixed at such a point that this full capacity will be utilized, or as much higher as may be necessary to pay the monopoly a fair profit on its operations.

This influence just considered has its origin in the selfishness of men. The second, and by far the most important influence tending to ameliorate the evils due to monopolies and intense competition arises from that essentially noble trait of human character whose province it is to seek the welfare of others before that of self. It is not to be wondered at that the large benevolence of our noblest Christian thinkers rebels against the inflexible laws of competition, or rather at their stern application to modern conditions of life. Under our social system, indeed, each man is striving to do his utmost to benefit his fellow-men, but only so far as it benefits himself. Christianity goes far beyond this. It teaches the Fraternity of Man, the Fatherhood of God, and thus the duty of all men to care for and love their brothers' happiness and welfare. It is in accord with the noblest and most exalted desires of the human soul. It teaches a man to seek to benefit others for their own sake, not for the sake of the reflex benefit on himself.

The burden of Christ's sermon on the mount was that golden rule of action,

"Whatsoever ye would that men should do to you, do ye even so to them"; and the whole of his teachings glow with the spirit of fraternity; the strong bearing the burdens of the weak; the rich cast down and the poor exalted; brother sharing with brother, according to their needs. We are accustomed to make ourselves complaisant with the reflection that these were figurative expressions, and not meant as literal commands. But if we consider candidly, we must confess that if it is the spirit of its Master's commands which the Church means to follow, it is very far, as a body, from reaching up to their full import. The love for one's fellow-men which Christ taught was certainly meant to be expressed in great, noble acts of brotherly kindness. Consider the want, the suffering, the distress, the misfortune, the inequality by which a thousand families have hard work and scanty fare while one revels in luxury. Are these thing repugnant to the spirit of Christianity, or not? Every one knows that they are. It is because Christian men in these days are prone to follow their own ease in common with the rest of the world, and are accustomed to make their Christian code of morals to fit that which public opinion declares to be sufficiently advanced, that Christianity as a remedy for social evils has fallen into disrepute with the laboring classes. But men, both in and out of the Church, who are better informed as to the grand and noble spirit that lies at its foundation, are coming to look more and more toward Christianity as the only deliverance from the evils that threaten us.

Our social system, say the devout among these men, is based on the selfish desires of men, their wish to get the most for themselves with the least service to their fellow-men. It is inconceivable that a system founded on any thing less than the noblest attributes of humanity can be intended as a permanent basis for society. The system founded on competition was adapted to the conditions of men during the formative period of civilization: but modern inventions, processes, and methods are revealing a strange want of elasticity in its action. It is leading us to such grave evils that men everywhere are looking for an escape from it. We are brought face to face with the fact that the law of competition, the cruelly terse "survival of the fittest," was never meant to control the wondrously intricate relations of the men of the coming centuries. And if selfishness is not to control, it is because unselfishness is to reign in its stead. It is because there will grow up in the hearts of men a fraternal love, such as the world has not yet seen, which will make them gladly share a common inheritance with each other, as they do a common Fatherhood. Men will then labor for others' welfare as now; but each with the thought of others' benefit, not of his own.

Nor are these men alone in their belief. Earnest thinkers outside of the Church, who are familiar with the evils which intense competition and extortionate monopoly are constantly pushing into our notice, discern a tendency in our social organism to pulsate with stronger and more rapid beats in its convulsions of strike and boycott and commercial crisis. And in these mighty vibrations, like the swing of a gigantic pendulum, there is danger that it may swing so hard and so far as to break its controlling bonds and leave humanity in chaos.

Anarchy means more than the reign of individualism. It means such a ruin of the world's wealth, the storehouses and fields and factories which supply its wants, that nine tenths of the population of the globe would be swept off its face by actual starvation. Some social organism there must be if our civilization is to continue. What can adjust the delicate relations of man to man when the bond of selfishness which holds us together breaks? There are many men, even now, whose greatest desire and strongest purpose is to benefit their fellow-men; and if we can extend and strengthen this noble principle so that it will govern the great mass of humanity, why may we not cease to measure and bargain and weigh with our brother men?

Such is the argument for what we may appropriately call Christian communism. Who shall say what shall be possible with a new and nobler generation of men? When the great mass of the race has Altruism for its governing motive, then it may be possible to use that trait of character as the basis of industrial society. But to-day the governing motives of mankind are largely selfish. Society must govern men in their dealings with each other, not by arbitrary force but by their inner motives of action. When men at large begin to heartily desire to benefit others more than themselves, then the system of selfish competition will begin to disappear, and the system of fraternal devotion will arise to take its place. This will come about naturally. It will be an effect which can only be brought about by producing the cause. When Christianity shall have so regenerated mankind that its governing motives are noble and generous, then the social problems we are discussing, as well as many others, will be forever happily solved.

Every one will say, God speed the attempt to implant such noble motives in the breasts of men; but we recognize at the same time the vast change which must be wrought before mankind at large will reach this high standard; and in the centuries which will be required to effect this, we must have other forces to govern society. Thus, while not denying the possibility that the Christian principle of Altruism may be the final solution of the problem of society, it seems best for us to regard it at the present day as what it is,--an influence tending to smooth over the inequalities and soften the asperities of our social system, and to transform the warfare of competition into a peaceable and friendly emulation.

It is not easy to overestimate the valuable work which this Christian principle of human fraternity is thus doing at the present day. It is recognized in many ways so common that we cease to think of them as what they are--expressions of the common brotherhood of man. Our vast public charities supported by law are an instance. It is recognized now by all civilized countries that it is a duty for the State to care for those who are so poor or unfortunate as to be unable to care for themselves. Private charities, too, are as much more enormous now than they were a century ago as private fortunes are, compared with those of that day. In fact, beneficence has come to be recognized as an important duty of the very wealthy; and churches, schools, hospitals, and the like bear witness everywhere to the benevolence of wealthy men. All this public and private benevolence has certainly accomplished wonderful results in relieving the want and misfortune of men, and making their lot a bearable one.

The above beneficences require outright giving; but there are many ways in which the fraternal spirit of men works to cause men to treat each other in business affairs more liberally than they would if competition were the only governing motive. In very many cases of the employment of labor, the wages paid are higher than the rate which competition alone would fix. It is true that this is largely due to a selfish motive. The men are more contented and industrious than when their wages are lower. There are always plenty of applicants for any vacant position. The men are not prone to find fault with their pay, knowing that plenty would be glad to fill their places. At the same time, it is certainly true that in many cases a principal motive for giving higher wages is the desire to be liberal and generous with the workers whose labor brings income and profits. Again it is very frequently the case that mills and mines are kept in operation in dull times, when goods must be sold at a loss, if sold at all, simply to keep the employees from the destitution and suffering consequent upon idleness. Cases of especial personal benevolence are still more common. There are tens of thousands of working people to-day rendering service whom their employers well know to be unprofitable servants, but who are retained because their youth or age or incapacity renders them proper objects of assistance in this way, a sort of charity far better than outright gift.

In business enterprises, again, the spirit of fraternity is widely diffused. As we have seen, it has been one principal cause of the formation of trusts and combinations to limit and restrain competition. There are also a growing number of enterprises which are purely philanthropic, such as the provision of cheap and healthy homes for working men and women.

In the conduct of business, too, public opinion does not approve of the man who exacts the utmost farthing, and weighs and measures to the closest fraction. The most grasping creditor, who precipitates the ruin upon the bankrupt, and the landlord or money-lender, who exacts pitilessly and turns a deaf ear to the call of a brother for mercy, are also condemned at the bar of public opinion.

These and many other considerations lead us to some knowledge of the inestimable value of the principle of fraternity to correct the harsh and inequitable working of the industrial organism. It remains only to be said that in this sphere of action its influence is but a small fraction of what it ought to be and what it promises to become.

It is through their conscience, as well as through their innate sense of justice and right, that men are coming to see how the extortion by monopolies and the waste of competition in which they have engaged are an injury to the common weal and an expression of might rather than of right. It is in this way that we are beginning to discern the faults and imperfections of our present industrial system and to recognize that progress toward better things is to be found by recognizing, not covering, these faults, and doing all in our power to remedy them. In this work the Christian Church should be in the lead; and a large proportion of its pastors, accustomed to an earnest and sympathetic appreciation of social evils, are among the foremost to second the efforts of modern reformers. Of the rank and file of the Church, however, it is to be regretfully said that they are eminently conservative; and that, with very many notable exceptions, they are certainly not in the lead in the efforts to equalize the injustices which have grown up under the laws of competition. It is largely because the course of Christians is in this respect so inconsistent with their professed belief in that grand doctrine of man's divine origin and universal brotherhood, that the Church, is losing the respect of the laboring classes. Nor will it regain that respect until it shows by unmistakable evidence to the men who toil with their hands that it is alive to the questions of the day,--alive to the injustice of society to-day; and that the love of the Church's great Master for their souls is echoed by a longing in the hearts of his followers for their temporal welfare.

But it should be also said that, save as they assume it, the responsibility of those within the Church is not greater than of those without. All men alike are brothers; and it is more, far more, than a selfish tie that binds us together in civilized society. Legal rights are based largely on the system of competition under which our industries have grown up; but the moral duties of all men go far beyond this. It is the duty of all men alike to supplement the working of the law of selfish competition with the acts of a fraternal love for the welfare of all men. Too much stress cannot be laid on this. There can be little doubt that if it were not for the charity and beneficence and for the strong spirit of humanity, which lives in a strange strength, even in the hearts of the debased and evil-minded, the industrial warfare which our modern competition has come to be would have wrought tenfold more evil than it has, and would have already arrayed class against class with other weapons than those of peaceable industry. May Heaven grant that the time shall never come when the growth of the principle of human fraternity shall not far outstrip and overtop the growth of human selfishness, whatever forms the latter may take.

In concluding this chapter it seems eminently proper to call attention to one practical application of this great principle of fraternity which ought to go a great way towards saving us from the results of mistakes in our attempts to remedy the evils which have grown up. The fraternal principle should lead men to judge charitably the men who are engaged in monopolies and in wasting the world's wealth in intense competition. The more especially as these evils are due, not to the malignity of any person, but to our system of industry, which causes them to spring up. The investigation which we pursued in the first chapters showed very clearly that monopolists are simply striving, like all other men, to protect and advance their own interests by what they consider legal and honorable means. And our study of the laws of competition has shown us that the evils of monopoly and unhealthy competition are the natural outgrowth of the great revolution in modern industries by which the number of competing units has been reduced from many to few.

Unfortunately there is a great tendency to make these evils worse by recrimination. It is very common to hear those engaged in monopolistic enterprises, whether as owners or managers, denounced as unscrupulous villains, double-dyed rascals, scoundrelly enemies of the people, or perhaps in terms less blunt but more scathing. Now, what are the facts of the case? Speaking broadly, it is a fact that the men who own and manage our modern monopolies are as a class far more large-hearted in their sympathies than the average of men. It is only because they do not realize the consequences of their acts that they seem to those who do realize them and those who suffer by them to be incomprehensibly brutal. The same man who at a corporation meeting may do his part toward throwing a thousand men out of employment or wasting a million dollars of the world's wealth to effect some monster "deal," may stop as he leaves his office to help a crippled beggar regain his feet; and when he hears of the destitution that his own official act has helped create, he will give with a lavish hand to relieve it. When we come to questions between labor and its employers, more than this is true. The employers of labor as a class are closely in sympathy with the honest desire of their men to better themselves, and the constant increase in the employment of arbitration to settle difficulties, the experiments in co-operation and profit-sharing, and the furnishing of cheap and good houses to the workers are all evidences of this fact.

The truth is, that it is circumstances, not men, which have created monopolies. For to tell the truth, there are but very few men who, if put in the place of the stigmatized monopolists, would not have done as much or more, as their abilities permitted, to achieve a fortune as have these men. All men strive in general to make as much as possible out of their fellow-men, and to gain the most possible with the least labor. The monopolist only goes further on this road than most other men can go.

On the other hand, a still more common error exists with reference to the monopolies of labor. The newspaper press seems strangely fond of repeating the statement that all labor organizations are kept up by idle and turbulent labor agitators, who wish to live off the proceeds of their fellows' labor. A little candid thought and investigation will convince any one that this is an out-and-out lie, and as such deserves the condemnation of all honest men. Granted, indeed, that labor monopolies are an evil, as we have fully shown, and that the men who have charge of them are far from perfect, and make many mistakes, they have far more to excuse them than have the men who form monopolies for the purpose of adding to fortunes already plethoric. The truth is, that if the men who are so incomprehensibly unjust in their estimate of the work of labor organizations were put in the place of the laborers at the bench or in the mill, they would be foremost in securing their own rights by organizing their fellow workmen. It would be a great thing for the world's peace if men would try to look at their brother's failings through their brother's eyes. Before you criticise a man too harshly, candidly consider whether you would do any better if you were in his place.

We hear much said of the folly and wickedness of stirring up and reviving the sectional animosity between the North and the South; and all patriotic men rejoice in burying past issues and inaugurating the era of a united nationalism. But those who, by personal attacks upon monopolists, whether they are millionaire monopolists or hard-handed workingmen, cultivate animosity and hatred between social classes already too widely separated and too prone to hostility, are sowing seed whose fruit may be reaped in a social strife far more destructive and fatal than any sectional strife could be. In discussing remedies for the evils we have been investigating, we should always keep the fact in mind that our remedy should seek, not to punish, but to cure. Personal or class enmities never yet helped the world to advance. It will be fortunate if men can be taught to see how useless such enmities are in this case; and how little revenge and reprisal can ever do to heal a wrong.

XIV.

REMEDIES FOR THE EVILS OF MONOPOLY.

We have now investigated the nature of all the different classes of monopolies and combinations for the suppression of competition. We have studied their working and their effect upon the different classes of society. We have discussed the foundation principles of civilized society as seen in abstract theory and as seen in the actual practice of to-day, with the evils which intense competition on the one hand and extortionate monopoly on the other have brought upon us. Finally, we have considered the influences which tend to lessen and ameliorate these evils, and the extent to which we may rely on them to benefit the condition of society. We are now fully prepared to consider the remedies which are proposed for these evils, and to see in what direction our hope lies for the improvement of the condition of mankind.

It would be a far larger task than we propose to attempt, however, to discuss all the schemes which have been proposed for bettering the condition of society. They have been numerous ever since the dawn of the idea of popular liberty, have accompanied it all through its centuries of growth, and to-day, despite the fact that the amount of the comforts of life accessible to the masses of the people is far greater than ever before, plans for further betterment of the condition of society, the more economical production and equitable distribution of wealth, are being pressed forward and advocated more strongly than ever. Nor does this fact furnish any ground for pessimism. We shall have far more occasion to deplore when men become so conceited over the advancement which the race has already made,--so numb to the evils which still oppress them,--that they will no longer take part in the agitation of plans for further advancement.

In considering now the plans proposed at the present day by those who wish to remedy the evils of monopoly, we shall find it profitable to consider first two great opposing principles, which we will designate as individualism and societism. Upon one or the other of these principles almost every scheme for bettering the condition of society is based.

The doctrine of individualism has for its foundation the absolute industrial liberty of each individual. By this is meant that every person shall have "the free right of contract,"--that is, the right to sell his labor or property or purchase that of others as he chooses. It holds that in all matters where the production and distribution of wealth is concerned, the desire of each man to advance his own interests will, alone, in the long run, result in the highest good to the greatest number. It asks the government to "let alone" the industrial affairs of the country, and leave private enterprise to take its own course. Its adherents are fond of asserting that each man knows his own wants and can direct his own business affairs much better than any government can direct them for him. It declares that free competition is the best possible agent to regulate all industrial affairs, and it ascribes all economic evils to the fact that free competition has been thwarted or destroyed.

The opposing doctrine of societism holds that the waste in the production of wealth and the inequities in its distribution, which afflict mankind to-day, are due to the extreme application of the doctrine of individualism. Its adherents analyze competition and declare it to be but another expression of a law of savage nature, tersely expressed as "the survival of the fittest." A system which brutally forces the weaker to the wall, say they, is unfit to govern the inter-relations of civilized human beings. Condemning thus the principles and practice of their opponents, they would go to the opposite extreme and place the control of the production and distribution of wealth in the hands of organized society or of local and central governments, to be by them administered for the common benefit.

The first and most obvious commentary upon these two opposing doctrines is that either of them is impracticable; and that if either of them were given the entire control of our industries, the whole people would unite in condemning it. Lest there should be any mistake as to what is meant by this, it is well to say that we now refer to neither the individualism nor the societism which is practically advocated at the present day, but rather to the essence of the two opposing principles.

To see most clearly the practical failure of either of these principles when applied without modification by the other, consider our present social system, which is based on both individualism and societism. If the principle of individualism were to be fully applied and societism were to be entirely abolished, a first step would be the relinquishment by the government of all the enterprises it now carries on; and they would be left for private enterprise to take up or leave alone as it chose. This means, for one thing, to bring the matter plainly home, that the whole national postal system would be wiped out, and we should depend on some private company or companies to collect, carry, and distribute our mails. The government would also abandon all its work in keeping clear and safe the natural waterways of the country, as well as all the harbors, light-houses, etc. Municipal governments would give up all their systems of water supply to private companies, as well as their sewerage systems, and even paving, street cleaning, etc. Indeed, the maintenance of our whole system of highways would be given over to private enterprise. Is this too much? It is only a legitimate application of the principle that government should leave to private enterprise all matters connected with commerce and industry.

Little need be said to prove that a similar application of the principle of societism to our industrial system would result even more disastrously. As a general thing, the necessary formality and expense of administration when business is carried on by the government, causes the final cost of production to be much greater than under private management, even when conducted with all honesty. But the chief reason why the principle of societism is impracticable and unwise for universal application, lies in the fact that the men who administer our governments are neither the wisest nor the most honest of men. The competition among those engaged in private business tends by a process of natural selection to bring the men of greatest business ability into control of affairs. But by any form of government yet tried, popularity rather than merit, and excellence in the arts of the politician, rather than experience and capacity as a statesman and business man, are the qualities which place men in positions where they can control public affairs. Not that very many wise and good men do not now hold office, and that many unprincipled and vicious men do achieve success in private business. But, as a general rule, the statements just made hold good.

It seems plainly apparent, then, that neither the principle of individualism nor the principle of societism can be taken as an infallible guide for determining the control of our industry. It would be as manifestly unwise to take a step toward abolishing existing societism by placing our postal department under the control of a private company, as it would be to make a move toward abolishing individualism by having the government assume the management of all the farms in the country. Both of these principles are necessary.

There is, indeed, a marked tendency toward an increased reliance on the principle of societism as civilization progresses and our life becomes necessarily more intense and complex. A community of plain farmers, isolated from each other, can live their individual lives about as they please, without any interference of the government becoming necessary to protect the rights of each man from infringement by his neighbors. But the resident in a large village must submit to certain restrictions for the common good. He must not carry on any kind of business likely to become a public nuisance. His cattle may not graze in the streets. He must give part of his earnings toward maintaining a water supply for a protection against fire. The citizen of a great city is subject to far more restrictions. The government assumes the control of education, charities, the care of the public health, the drainage of the streets, the collection of offal, and a multitude of other duties which in a less intense civilization each family performs for itself.

The advance in science and the arts, too, has brought about a revolution whose effect we must recognize. A hundred years ago almost every community, and to a large degree every family, was industrially almost independent of every other, as we have already shown. To-day each man relies on a million others to supply him with the commonest necessaries of life. The armored knight was proof against all foes, save the few antagonists similarly clad. To-day my life is dependent on the fidelity and vigilance of ten thousand men, and every man I meet has me in his power. Given the malignant will and fiendish cunning necessary, and one single man can kill a thousand human beings and destroy a million dollars at a blow. To sum up, each advance in civilization makes men more dependent upon each other, and increases the advantage and necessity of having industries most important to the common welfare controlled by society as a whole instead of by individuals.

It is contended by some that from the increased interference of government with private affairs, there is danger that the liberties of the people will be curtailed, and that their rights will be so hedged about by restrictions that the result will be evil instead of beneficial. To this it must be answered that the people themselves are the source of the government's authority and power of restriction, and that in no case will a restriction of the government be long maintained which does not benefit far more in conserving the rights of men than it injures by infringing them. Apply this rule to any case of government action in industrial matters. A city government, for instance, constructs a system of sewerage. All taxpayers must contribute something towards its expense, and their right to spend that money in such other ways as they choose is abridged; but, at the same time, the more important right of having healthy and safe drainage for their houses is conserved. In a similar way, the government may pass laws of various sorts to restrict and control what seems to be at first sight purely private business, such as the sale of explosives, spirituous liquors, poisons, drugs, and many other articles. In every instance, this is done on the ground that the interference of government is necessary to protect the rights of the community as a whole, even though the liberties of certain classes are abridged.

The study of these facts brings to our attention an important principle of governmental action, which should always be remembered when in any industrial matter we find that the principle of individual action is producing unsatisfactory results, and conclude, therefore, to ask the government to take some part in its control. This principle is as follows: government, as the representative of the will of the whole people, should in general, attempt the regulation, or control, of industrial matters only to benefit the people as a whole.

Of course it cannot be said that all government action for the benefit of special classes of the community is wrong. The granting of pensions to those defenders and upholders of the government who deserve it, is a case in point where special legislation is justifiable and proper; and many other cases exist. Nevertheless, the shaping of legislation to effect the interests of special classes of the community is one which is now working the nation serious injury; and it has obtained so firm a bold that it will take a long time for us to throw it off. It causes men of all classes to consider the government as a paternal benefactor, whose duty it is to aid them, either in their schemes for getting rich or their struggles to earn a living; when its real office is to protect all citizens in their individual rights, undertake only such industrial enterprises as can manifestly be better and more economically conducted by it than by private enterprise, and enforce restrictions upon industry only as they are needed to protect personal rights or the interests of the community as a whole. Worst of all, the use of government to advance special interests places a premium on the efforts of those who seek to corrupt the expression of the popular will in its every stage, from the voters at the polls to the chief rulers in the seats of government. For by combining to accomplish their mutual purposes, they are able to turn aside all departments of government from their legitimate work and occupy them with measures to advance special interests, some commendable enough, others a mere excuse for stealing from the public treasury, but all alike claiming attention and action, while the business of the people goes all awry.

It has seemed necessary to thus briefly discuss these two opposing theories of society, individualism and societism, in order to show the impracticability of either when applied to the society of to-day without limitation and modification by the other; and that in adopting or rejecting any remedies that may be proposed for the industrial evils which we have discussed, we should be guided by the facts as we find them, and not by blind adherence to abstract principles.

Let us now gather up the salient decisions which we have reached in all our past investigation. We have discovered that a great industrial revolution is in progress, by which manufacturing, mining, and transportation to a very great extent, and other industries to a considerable extent, have been and are being concentrated in the hands of a very few competitors. We have found that by the laws of competition this reduction in the number of competitors greatly increases the intensity of competition and the resulting waste and instability of price, and finally brings monopoly into existence. This monopoly we have determined to be a serious infringement on the rights of the people, and we have found that the losses due to intense competition and the fruitless attempts to defeat monopoly by adding new competing units have wasted the wealth of the nation in uncounted millions. We are now to consider the remedies proposed for these evils.

The most obvious remedy for monopoly, and the one which has been tried and persevered in with the most remarkable faith, is the creation of new competitors. Does a railroad monopoly oppress us? Build a competing line. Is the gas company of our city charging us $3 per thousand for gas which cost but 50 cents to produce and deliver? Let us start another gas company and tear up all our pavements again to lay its mains. Has the sugar trust put up the price of sugar two cents per pound? Well, "sugar can be produced anywhere by the expenditure of labor and capital," the Trust's lawyers say, and so we will "trust" that some enterprising manufacturer will take the field against the combination. But if we do any of these things, we have added only one competitor to the number in the field. And with only two competitors in the field, competition is sure to be so intense and wasteful that the formation of a new monopoly is a matter of but a short time.

This is the conclusion to which the theory brings us; and the more one studies the history of actual attempts to create competition in this way, the more thoroughly convinced he must be that the inevitable result will be the same,-- the tacit or formal combination between the old monopoly and the new competitor, resulting in the re-establishment of the absolute reign of monopoly. The author has thoroughly studied the actual working of hundreds of schemes, in every part of the United States, whose object was to create competition in railroad transportation. It is a most astonishing fact to see the eagerness with which thousands of municipalities, all over the country, which have taken great loads of debt upon their shoulders to secure "competing lines," and have seen these lines swallowed up by their rivals, are still anxious to repeat the folly and assume new burdens to aid in building new lines, which will inevitably be absorbed like those which they preceded. If the people as a whole learn wisdom by experience, they seem to learn with painful slowness. The first great lesson for the people who are groaning under the burden of monopoly to learn, then, is that when we try to defeat monopoly by creating new competing units, the remedy is worse for the community at large than the disease, and effects at best but a temporary relief.

Another class of remedies against monopoly seek to accomplish their purpose by opposing the tendency to a reduction in the number of competing units. There are not wanting people who, having gained a dim perception that monopolies are an inevitable result of the modern concentration of industry, conclude that, after all, "the former days were better than these," and that our wisest course is a retrograde one. Fortunately, however, these people are comparatively few. It is a fact so plain that even the dullest can hardly fail to perceive it, that the consolidation and concentration of industry which have gone on everywhere have wonderfully cheapened the cost of production,-- made it possible for us to make better goods with a less expenditure of labor and material. The revolution in our industries could not be undone without a more radical action toward vested property rights than could be countenanced now; and as already seen, it would work to the detriment of every person in the community. We cannot go back to the stage-coach, the workshop, and the hand-loom of our ancestors; we cannot, if we would, undo the growth of a century in civilization; and it is well that it is so.

But while most men see the benefit which has resulted from the consolidations already effected, there are but few who are not opposed to further consolidations. It is argued that the reduction in the number of competing units results in increasing the intensity of competition, which is assumed to be a desirable end; and that it has also worked great benefit in the reduction in cost. Having attained this, it is proposed to stop further consolidations and prevent the establishment of monopoly. This is what most of the present plans for giving relief from monopoly propose to accomplish. Certainly the task is no easy one; let us inquire if it be even possible.

We may safely assume, in the first place, that the competitors in any industry will always be reduced to a very small number before the public will be sufficiently aroused to make any movement for the prevention of consolidation. So long as a monopoly is not imminent, usually, indeed, so long as it is not in actual operation, no one cares or notices how far consolidation and combination goes. Now by the laws of competition, when the number of competing units is small, competition is intense and wasteful, and acts to so reduce the returns from industry that combination and the establishment of a monopoly are a natural sequence.

Evidently this result can only be prevented by some interference outside the industry itself. If we allow it to take its own course, a monopoly is certain, sooner or later, to be formed. But the only agency which has the right and power to interfere is government. The question then is, can government successfully interfere to prevent intense competition from bringing about monopoly? In order to do this it must of course keep competition in action; but it cannot do this directly. Competition is essentially a strife. No law was ever enacted which could force two men to fight if they were really determined to be at peace. No law was ever enacted which could force two manufacturers or merchants to compete with each other in price, if they really were agreed to sell at the same price. The common-law principle that contracts in restraint of competition are void, so often appealed to nowadays, has really but slight power. It merely prevents the parties who make an agreement to restrain competition, from enforcing such agreements in court. Attempts have also been made to apply this principle to secure an annulment of the charter of corporations which engage in monopolistic combinations. Even if this be successful, the only result probable is that private parties instead of corporations will carry on the monopolies in a few cases, while in most cases the competition-destroying agreements will be made so secretly that it will be impossible to prove their existence.

It is thus plain that the action of the government in declaring the restriction of competition to be illegal is wholly ineffectual to check the growth of monopoly. And, further, the fact is that it is hardly possible for the government to take any more extreme stand in the matter. Let us suppose that it does declare, not only that these combinations are against public policy, but that they shall be punished. Then would it be a punishable offence for two country grocers who had been selling sugar below cost to agree that henceforth they would charge a uniform price and make an eighth of a cent per pound! It is to be remembered that competition necessitates action. Can the government, therefore, compel a man to compete, to cut prices below his neighbors, or to carry on his business at all, if he does not choose to do so? Such a law would establish the government's right to regulate the conduct of purely private business to a degree never before known. Such a law to protect the theory of individualism would be a most flagrant infringement of the rights of individuals. It is plain, then, that government cannot possibly keep up competition by direct action.

Whether it is possible to do so by indirect means is a much harder question. Monopoly results, as we have found, from the intensity of competition. If it is possible to modify the intensity, to keep the candle from burning itself out too quickly, so to speak, it is possible that competition may be kept alive by legislative enactment. So far, practically nothing has been done in this direction, and it remains yet to be seen what remedies of this sort may accomplish.

A pertinent example of an attempt by the government to keep competition alive is the Interstate Commerce law. Before its passage the railway companies had a patched-up and nominally illegal species of combination to restrict competition, known as pooling. As described by President Charles Francis Adams of the Union Pacific Railway, "it was merely a method through which the weaker corporations were kept alive." The Interstate law prohibited this restriction of competition, and also, by enactment of the long-and short-haul clause, made the competition more widespread and injurious to the railways. As a result an astonishing impetus has been given to the growth of the great systems and the consolidation of the minor competing roads. More than that, however, the great increase in the intensity of competition has done so much to drain the resources of the companies and injure their revenues, that some measure for uniting all the railroads of the country under one management is now being seriously planned by many men in railroad circles. Thus this result, which was probably inevitable, has doubtless been hastened many years by the action of the law. The means taken to intensify competition has operated, as might have been expected, to hasten the complete establishment of monopoly.

We have now found that monopoly is the inevitable result of the concentration of competition in any industry in a few hands, if events are allowed to take their natural course; that the only agent which has either the right or the power to interfere in the case is the government,--National, State, or Municipal; that government cannot punish directly those who form combinations to restrict competition, without exercising to an unprecedented degree its right to interference with private affairs; while its attempt to deter men from establishing monopolies by refusing its protection to them in their contracts to restrict competition has proved to be but a slight hindrance to the growth of monopoly.

There are, then, but two ways of preventing monopoly from establishing itself and laying such a tax upon the people at large for the supply of the commodity which it controls as it chooses. The first is, action to reduce the intensity of competition so that the weaker competitors may maintain their independence and not be forced to consolidate with their stronger rivals. The second is, action to permit or encourage the establishment of monopoly, and regulate by some means other than competition the prices which it shall charge for the products and the quality of product which it shall supply. These two general classes of remedies which we find to be feasible we will discuss here only in a general way. The first, reduction in the intensity of competition, has hardly been tried in any form, and we cannot yet say what practical means should be taken to put it into effect. We will return to this at a later period in our discussion.

The second remedy is the one towards whose adoption we are rapidly working. State and Interstate Commissions have already been established to regulate railway monopolies; and in general it is true that the people who feel the burden of monopolies are looking to the government for relief, and expect it to take positive action for the control of other monopolies as it has for the control of railways. It will be seen that we have now arrived by a study of the various possible remedies for monopoly at the same irresistible conclusion to which we were brought by our study of the laws of competition. The proper remedy for monopoly is not abolition but control. It seemed necessary to conduct this independent investigation in order that no blind adherence to individualism and no thought of the possible efficacy of other remedies might lead us to doubt this important truth.

We have next to consider the fact that the government can control monopolies in two ways. It can either permit the monopoly to remain under private ownership, and regulate its operations by law and by duly appointed officers; or it can itself assume the entire ownership and control of the monopoly. Which of these plans is the better, is a question of public policy over which future political parties are likely to dispute. One party will hold that when it is necessary for the government to interfere to protect those whom it represents from the oppression of monopoly, it should assume at once the whole ownership and management of the monopoly. Their opponents will argue that government should interfere only to the extent needful to maintain the rights of the public; and that it is far better that industry should be directed by the private individuals whose interests are at stake than by government officials. To discuss fully the arguments for each of these two principles of our future practice in dealing with monopolies, would be beyond the intended scope of this volume. It can only be briefly said that the arguments presented will certainly indicate that the conditions surrounding each given monopoly will have great weight in determining which policy is the most advantageous. It would be manifestly unwise, for instance, to place our postal facilities under the direction of a corporation, even though its operations were regulated by government. It would be even more unwise to place the operations of the flouring mills of the country in the hands of a department of the government. The important factors to be considered in deciding any given case are, first, the importance and necessity to the public of the service, and, second, the question whether production in the given case is likely to be carried on more economically by the government or by private enterprise. The former has an advantage in that it can secure its capital at a lower rate of interest. The latter, an advantage in that it secures greater efficiency from the labor it employs. Other circumstances being equal, it would appear wisest, then, for government to take direct charge of those monopolies in which the greatest amount of capital is invested and the least labor is employed, leaving to private enterprise under government regulation the operation of monopolies in which the opposite set of conditions prevails.

As already stated, however, the question is complicated by the social and industrial effects which might follow a large transfer of enterprise from private to governmental direction; and these effects we will not now discuss.

XV.

THE SOVEREIGN RIGHTS OF THE PEOPLE AND OF THEIR REPRESENTATIVE, THE GOVERNMENT.

We have now at last deduced the important facts, that the only remedy for the evils of monopoly must come from the popular will, expressed in direct action by the government; that the government may possibly keep competition alive by checking its intensity, or can certainly allow events to take their natural course and permit monopolies to be established. It can then protect the public, either by assuming itself the ownership and operation of the monopoly, or by taking the less radical step of placing the monopoly under official supervision and control while permitting its private ownership to continue. This conclusion is of the utmost importance, for it marks out one single direction as the one in which relief from the evils which vex us may be found. If we can once make the thinking people of the country understand the effect which monopolies have upon their welfare, and that the evil will not cure itself and cannot be cured by attempts to create competition or by any remedy short of direct action by the government, we shall have made a great advance.

But with this goal reached, new questions at once present themselves. Can the interference of the government with private industries be defended? How shall government exercise its control, so as to protect the people without infringing vested property rights and discouraging private enterprise? It may be objected, too, that, while our preceding discussion has fully proved the weakness of other methods of dealing with monopoly, compared with that by the direct action of government, it has not been shown that the latter is practicable, or that it would not be likely to result in more harm than good to the people at large.

These questions are coming before the people in a thousand practical forms. They are being fought over in courts and legislatures and councils, and are destined to be fought over at the polls. How important their right decision is, we have already seen. Let us make some attempt to find what this right decision is.

In taking up first the question of the rights of private property holders, we touch a point over which there is likely in the future to be serious dispute. A certain faction vigorously contend that past precedents are no ground on which to base future action, and that little attention need be paid to the rights of private owners if the public interest is at stake. A far stronger and more influential faction are jealous of every thing which seems to question their right to hold and use their property in whatever way they see fit. But certainly, if their claims are just, they need not fear the result of that investigation which every idea we have inherited from former generations has in these days to receive. It would be beyond the scope of our investigation to make any exhaustive study of this subject, but it is necessary to note some of the important facts in connection with property rights as light upon the question at issue.

In the first place, it must be conceded that the question is to be decided upon its merits, and not by precedent. It is of little use for one faction to show, as they can, that the idea of private property is largely of modern growth; or for their opponents to prove, as they may, that the progress of law and government has been continually toward better protection of the rights of property. The question must be, on what grounds of inherent right or public expediency is property held to-day in private ownership? Distasteful as it may be, to realize that what has been considered a fundamental principle of civilized society is here challenged and put upon the defensive, the fact remains that the defence must be made, and must be based only on what is just and wise to-day, for the opposing side may properly reject arguments based on the wholly different conditions under which past generations lived.

The question of the rights of property in the products of labor we may pass briefly, as it is almost undisputed; and while certain thinkers have asserted that there is no such thing as a natural right to the ownership of property of any sort, it seems certain that this is true only in a technical sense; and that a man's right to hold, control, dispose of, and enjoy the fruits of his own strength or skill is as certain as his right to "life, liberty, and the pursuit of happiness," and follows from that right as a natural sequence. The most radical revolutionist hardly ventures nowadays to argue against this fact. Thus, though it is recognized that private property even in one's own strength and skill must, at times, be subjected to the higher law of public necessity--as when in time of war a man may be obliged to give up his time, strength, and even life for the public welfare--in general the right to hold the results of labor as private property is well established, on the grounds both of natural right and public expediency.

But when we consider the private ownership of the gifts of Nature and of public franchises, it is apparent that we are on very different ground. These forms of property, which constitute a great proportion of the world's total wealth, are not created by labor. Nature's gifts were not stored up to enrich and benefit any one man, but the whole race. It follows, therefore, that they are always, in the first instance, public property.

The argument presented to prove any inherent right of the private owners to any form of natural wealth seem to be insufficient to prove the case. The fact seems to be that the inherent right to the benefit of every one of Nature's gifts is vested, if perfect equity were established, in the whole human race; or, as a reasonable approach to this, in that portion of the public to whom this gift is a direct benefit. The title which the public holds may be transferred to private individuals, as a matter of expediency; but the public must still retain a prior claim upon the property. Its right to have the property used for the general welfare, transcends the right of any private owner to direct it solely to his own profit and the public injury.

It is thus plain that the private ownership of our natural wealth and of all public franchises rests on the grounds of expediency alone. All the lands and mineral wealth, all franchises for railway lines and for the various public works discussed in the chapters on municipal monopolies were the heritage of the whole people in the first instance, and they have only transferred the title to private owners because it seemed expedient so to do. On the grounds of expediency alone, then, is the private ownership of natural wealth to be considered.

It can hardly be doubted that in the case of our own country, the transfer to private owners of the title to our natural resources has been in the past the wisest and only proper course. It is a fact not often realized that the title to nearly all the natural wealth of the country, almost all the lands and mines and forests, has been held directly by the public within a century, and that the transfer to private owners of a great part of it has taken place within a generation.

The question now comes: Did the public, in transferring the title to a private owner, relinquish all its right to the future control of these valuable properties, as a private owner would have done? The answer must be in the negative. Regarded simply as a matter of expediency, it is plain that to cause the act of any public official to bind all succeeding generations, living under dissimilar conditions and circumstances, which were then unknown and unprophesied, might result in unbearable evils. Necessary as it might be at the start to give away valuable properties to meet present needs, one generation or its representatives has no conceivable right to sell for a mess of pottage the heritage of all succeeding ones. The fact is, then, that the natural title to all gifts of Nature is vested in the public at large; and while it is in duty bound to observe the contracts which it makes with private parties, it is also not to be thought that the dishonesty or incompetence of a public official, or the failure to foresee the future, can work for too long a time an injury to the community.

It seems certain that, in every case where the public has transferred to private owners the title to any gift of Nature, or has conferred any franchise upon a corporation, under whatever conditions, the right of supreme control still remains with the natural owner, the public; and when the need arises, this control may be exercised. The rights of the owners and the contract obligations into which the public has entered should be regarded so far as possible; but when the public necessity demands, control on its behalf can always be exercised.

This may seem like a formidable and revolutionary doctrine, but, in reality, it is based on every-day acts of the public representatives, with which every one is familiar. Suppose it is conceived to be for the public interest that a certain railway shall be built. To do this it is necessary to cross many hundred tracts of land, the title to which was many years ago transferred by the public to private owners who have bought and sold since then as they pleased, as if their control were absolute. Many of the owners of these lands may be opposed to parting with the right of way necessary for a railroad, but their private wishes must not stop the progress of improvements necessary to the general welfare. The State, which has the natural title, asserts its right to supreme control; and, if necessary, will use all its power to force these private owners to relinquish their land for the public good. This is the commonest example of the exercise of the right of eminent domain, but other cases frequently occur. The laying out of city streets, building public bridges, and, in fact, highways of every class, furnish a similar example. Provision of public water supply often requires an exercise of this power even more positive than in the cases just cited. By the construction of one great reservoir to store the flow of the Croton water-shed for the supply of New York City, it is proposed to condemn the dwellings and lands now owned and occupied by several thousand people. It is to be noted that, in every case, the rights of the private owners are observed, and compensation is made them for the damage done.

Under the common law the owner of lands bordering a running stream has certain rights to its use; and these riparian rights, as they are called, have been established by precedent for centuries. But, in the State of Colorado, it was found that the water in the streams was of such value for irrigation that the old system of permitting private ownership of these riparian rights led to grave abuses. The State Constitution, therefore, declares that all water in running streams is the inalienable property of the whole people, and the system providing for its use by private parties is based on this principle.

So much for the power of the public to exercise its supreme control, when public exigency requires, over Nature's gifts in land and water. As an example of the supreme control of the public over the franchises which it grants, take the case of the railway again. It is well established that the public has the right through its legal representatives to regulate the management and operation of the railway in every detail; and not only that, but the rates which the railway may charge for its services as well. Many other examples might be given, for the necessities of the present decade have awakened men as never before to the facts which we have just discussed. The final conclusion must inevitably be that the public as the sole possible holder of the natural title to the gifts of Nature, while it may find it expedient to transfer this ownership to private owners, retains always supreme control, which may be exercised as the public exigency demands.

We have next to determine in what cases the exercise by the public of this right of supreme control over its heritage is demanded. We are greatly aided here, however, by the thorough study we have made of the laws of competition. It is evident at once that competition in the case of natural agents acts according to the laws already found. Agricultural land in this country is so abundant and its ownership is so widely diffused that any monopoly of it is now impossible. Each farmer competes with every other farmer, and the extension of transportation facilities has so broadened the field of competition that in no industry is the day when the few competing units shall replace the many, and monopoly shall ensue, farther off than in this. In Great Britain and Ireland opposite conditions prevail. A limited amount of land is held by a few owners, and its rental is fixed without competition; consequently the land question has been almost, if not quite, the chief issue in British politics during this decade.

If we examine Nature's gifts to the world in the shape of metals, we find iron to be so widely distributed that competition has always acted to reduce profits, and that combinations to restrict competition in the production of the metal have only recently become even possible. On the other hand, the workable deposits of copper are so scarce and the number of competitors in its production is so much smaller, that it has become the subject of the greatest monopoly the world has ever seen.

With these examples--and any number of others might be cited--is it not plain enough that the laws of competition are exactly applicable to aid in solving the problem? The smaller the number of competing units, the stronger the tendency to monopoly. Certain gifts of Nature are given to us in profusion. The people transfer the title to private owners, and of these there must of necessity be so many that they will compete steadily with each other. The consequence is that the people receive the benefit from the country's natural resources, while the private owner gets only enough to compensate him reasonably well for the labor he employs and the capital which he invests. Certain other gifts of Nature are, as we have found, very scarce; the number of men who can own and use them and compete with each other in offering their advantages to the public is necessarily small. The inevitable result of this condition is, first, intense competition and then monopoly.

It is thus evident that there is no necessity for the State to interfere with the private ownership of those gifts of Nature which are so widely distributed that competition can act for the protection of the public. As regards those other gifts which are so limited in their extent that their control has become a matter of monopoly, the right of the public to exercise its control is already proven. Whether in any given case the exigency is so great as to call for the assertion of this power, is a question which must be decided in each case separately.

It may be objected, with truth, that nothing short of the actual ownership of all Nature's gifts by the public is in accord with absolutely perfect justice; but as a matter of fact every human work carried out by human hands and brains is only an approach to perfection. It will never be possible by any human agency to distribute the wealth production of the world with absolute equity. A careful writer says: "The view that the right of every human being to his share in the gifts of Nature should be recognized is not an unreasonable one." But by no system possible of putting into practical execution can these gifts be equitably divided among all men. What can be done is to cause the benefit of these gifts to be widely distributed, and to prevent them from being monopolized for the benefit of a few.

The fact maybe alluded to, that even under widespread competition the holders of the most favorably situated and richest lands, mines, etc., receive a benefit which in absolute equity should be divided among all men. But the vastly more important matter of the monopolies which prevent the public from obtaining the benefit of the natural resources to which it holds an inalienable title, so overshadows such trivial injustices that they may be neglected. So much attention has been called of late, however, to the fact that land as a gift of Nature should, if absolute justice were done, have the benefit from its use equally divided among all men, that something further on this subject may be said.

Let us first note the fact, which no one will dispute, that the title held by the public refers only to the "site value." The value of all improvements which are the product of labor belongs to the owner by natural right. Now it is conceivable that of the total value of $10,197,000,000 at which the farms of the United States were valued at the last census, $7,000,000,000 may perhaps have been the value of the land apart from the value of the buildings and improvements made since the country was settled. In 1880 there were at least 3,500,000 farmers who owned agricultural lands. It is a well-known fact that the holding of agricultural land in large parcels is the rare exception. We may reasonably conclude, therefore, that the "site value" held by each farmer was about $2,000. This is the sum which in absolute equity is said to belong to the public at large. But let us reflect that each farmer has only received a small proportion of this $2,000 through the increase in the value of his land. The fact is that the land which at first was actually valueless has increased in value with each generation, and it is this increase alone, apart from the increase due to the betterments, after which the public has any right to inquire. Remembering the number of sales and changes in the ownership which take place in this country, how often the benefits which have accrued to a single property are divided up among a number of heirs, and that each owner represents on the average a family of three individuals, it seems reasonable to suppose that this increase in the "site value" of each farm may have been divided among twenty different persons. Thus, while the statement may be made that the public has a claim upon the farms of the country of $7,000,000,000, it must be remembered that this sum has been divided among about 70,000,000 different people, and that this division has been in progress for over two centuries. When the benefits of our natural resources are so widely distributed as this, there can be little occasion to alarm ourselves regarding injustice through the private control of farming lands.

This, however, is somewhat apart from our argument. The main point, of which we must not lose sight, is that the private ownership of those gifts of Nature which are widely distributed operates to the general benefit of the community far more than any system of public ownership that could be devised. But, on the other hand, in the case of natural agents limited in amount, it is practically certain that sooner or later a monopoly will be established by their private owners, to the serious detriment of the public at large. The sovereign right of the public in this latter case to take such steps as are necessary for its proper protection, is something which both a priori reasoning and judicial decisions amply prove.

The great problem of monopoly would be a far easier one to solve, both theoretically and practically, were it as easy to regulate justly those forms of monopoly whose strength lies in combination only, as it is those whose power depends on the possession of gifts of Nature, which we have just considered. In dealing with trusts, monopolies in trade, and labor monopolies, we are in danger, on the one hand, of sanctioning oppressive interference with private business, and on the other of permitting a license in the conduct of private business which encourages its managers to continue to extort unjust gains from the public. In the face of this difficulty, which careful consideration shows to be very serious, and in the dread of other evils, such as the government proving incompetent to safely undertake these new and strange responsibilities, we may well feel like trying to get along with the aid of those old defenses against monopolies that have always, until the modern concentration of industry was accomplished, been ample to hold them in check.

But the one argument which prevents this is the fact that this tendency to concentration and consolidation is still actively at work. In the words of Prof. Ely: "Production on the largest possible scale will be the only practical mode of production in the near future." It is for this reason that we must not cease to look about for some better protection against this new class of monopolies than are afforded by merely placing stumbling-blocks in their way. We shall have need, for many years yet, of such weapons in fighting monopoly as the public is already familiar with; the creation of new competitors and their support by public opinion, judicial decisions against combinations, and the like. But before these grow absolutely useless, we ought to be prepared to meet the new conditions of industry with something better than mere opposition; and even now be experimenting and studying upon a permanent and consistent policy.

In attempting to control monopolies which are not dependent on natural agents for their strength, we are met at once by the declaration that the government has no power or right to interfere with property which is the product of labor; and that the owner cannot be prevented from making such disposition of it as he chooses. The President and Counsel of the Sugar Trust said after Judge Barrett's decision was announced: "We do not believe that the law prevents two persons engaged in rivalry with each other from uniting their interests." This seems indeed true; and yet, on reflection, it appears to be absolutely certain that power must reside in the sovereign people to protect themselves from the unjust taxation which a monopoly may seek to enforce. Let us brush away cobwebs and set the facts clearly before us. That competition among producers is the sole present protection of the public against extortionate prices is undoubted. When by combination this defense is abolished, has not the public a right to adopt some other means of protection? There can be no doubt that it has; the only question is, what form should that protection take?

It must be plain that, as a general rule, it is unfitting that government should own and operate industrial establishments. Practical experience has indicated that this experiment is wellnigh certain to result in failure, for reasons so evident as to require no mention here. The only alternative remaining is government regulation with private ownership and management. The essential features in the adoption of any plan should be that the returns of the private owner should be in proportion to the skill and economy which he exercises in managing his business; that competition and its resulting waste be done away with; and that the industry be placed on such a safe and stable basis that the capital invested in it shall receive the lowest possible rate of interest, thus leaving the greatest possible amount for the payment of wages of labor and permitting sales of the product at a low price.

XVI.

PRACTICAL PLANS FOR THE CONTROL OF MONOPOLIES.

The investigation of the preceding chapters, leading up to the final conclusion that the proper and only wise remedy for the evils of monopoly lies in direct action of the government to protect the rights of the people, finishes the chain of our argument and really accomplishes the work laid out in the opening chapter. The laws which we have found to govern competition in modern industry are so far-reaching in their effects, and their correct apprehension by the people at large is so important to the general welfare, that economists ought to unite in recognizing and teaching their truth, while all who desire to work for the alleviation of present crying evils of society should understand these laws and be guided by them.

In the practical application of these truths, however, so many complicated details are involved that there is ample reason for the widest differences of opinion. To decide intelligently upon these practical methods demands special knowledge, in order that all necessary details may be provided for, and rare practical judgment to adapt the method to the means at hand.

The investigations which the author has pursued in the preparation of the preceding chapters and for certain other purposes have suggested to him certain principles in the practical execution of plans for the control of various monopolies, which seem to him necessary to success in the work. Well understanding the fallibility of any one man's judgment, especially in these matters of detail, he has determined to outline in a brief way what seem to him the most feasible plans for the control of each class of monopolies. These suggestions, however, are to be regarded in an entirely different light from the general laws propounded in the preceding chapters; and they are presented with a full knowledge of the fact that slight variations in circumstances may necessitate wide changes in plans and processes.

Taking up the monopolies which by their use of natural agents or their exercise of a franchise granted by the public, are already acknowledged to be subject to the public control, let us consider first the railway system. The two years in which the Interstate Commerce law has been in force have seen a great progress toward the final solution of this problem, even though railway affairs are at present in so unsatisfactory a condition. The important features of our future policy which now seem to be quite generally understood are: full State and national control over both tariff rates and facilities; the abolition of competition, either by consolidation or by legalized agreements to that end; and strict prohibition of the construction of parallel lines not warranted by the traffic.

That we are working very rapidly in this direction, no one will deny who is familiar with the progress of legislation affecting railway interests and with the opinions of railway men. Evidently, however, government cannot justly take so prominent a part in railway management without becoming in some degree responsible to railway stock- and bond-holders for the protection of their interests; and it is a difficult question to say in what manner this responsibility should be met. It has been the intention of the author in devising the following plan for the control of our railway system to make this responsibility a definite one, and not leave it as now, a vague constitutional right. For according to the law at present, State and national legislators may make laws to vary the receipts and expenditures of the railway companies as much as they please, and the only redress of the railway owner is an appeal to the courts, the judges of which must decide whether the company's revenue is so injured that its legal rights are infringed.

Space will not permit here a full statement of the many serious evils and abuses with which our present system of railway management is burdened. The study which the author has made of them has convinced him of their importance and magnitude. The following plan is designed to permit their remedy as well as to remedy the special evils of monopoly with which our present investigation is concerned:

Let the government acquire the title to the franchise, permanent way, and real estate of all the railway lines in the country. Let a few corporations be organized under government auspices; and let each, by the terms of its charter, receive a perpetual lease of all the railway lines built or to be built within a given territory. Let the territory of each of these corporations be so large and so planned with regard to its neighbors that there shall be, so far as possible, no competition between them. For instance, one corporation would operate all lines south of the Ohio and east of the Mississippi rivers; another all lines east of the Hudson and of Lake Champlain, etc. Let the terms of rental of these lines be about 3?per cent. on the road's actual "present cost" (the sum of money it would cost to rebuild it entirely at present prices of material and labor) less a due allowance for depreciation. The corporations would be obliged to keep the property in as good condition as when received, and would own absolutely all their rolling stock, machinery, etc.

It is not proposed, however, that the government shall own any interest in the railways save the legal title. Bonds would be issued to the full amount of the appraised valuation, running twenty-five years and bearing interest at 3 per cent., principal and interest guaranteed by the government, and these would be sold to the highest bidder. Thus the real ownership of the roads would be vested in the bondholders. As is well known, there is a great and fast increasing need for investments of absolute safety, even though they bear very low rates of interest. This is especially desirable for the continuance of our national banking system, in order to insure us a safe, stable, and ample currency. Such bonds would find a market at a premium as fast as offered.

It would not even be necessary that the money to pay the interest coupons should pass through the government's hands. The operating company would pay it directly to the bond-holder and at the same time the ?of 1 per cent. would be paid into the government treasury.

The object in making the bonds run for no longer time than twenty-five years, when it is intended that the whole value of the road shall be perpetually held in the form of bonds, is that at proper intervals a revaluation may be made of the improvements to the road and the interest charges may be readjusted to correspond with the general change in the income from capital. When the bonds fall due, a new block would be issued and sold to the highest bidder. The interest rate should be set at such a point that the bonds could be sold at a premium. These premiums, with the ?of 1 per cent. on the bonds, paid by the operating company to the government, (which we may regard as a legitimate fee to the government for its guaranty) should form a government railway fund. This should be used, first, to defray the expenses of the government department of railways, and second, to pay the deficit when on any line the net receipts after operating expenses are paid are insufficient to pay the rental. The remainder should be expended in making improvements and additions to the railway system, such as building new bridges and stations, and improving the line, the cost of which, however, should be represented by additional bonds at the end of the twenty-five-year term. The amount of income should be so regulated, by varying the rate of interest on new bonds, that the sum remaining for the last purpose may be about sufficient for usual needs. The whole administration of the receipt and expenditure of this fund should be vested in the government department of railways. In this way the danger that the whole work of this government department might be blocked through the neglect of Congress to make necessary appropriations, would be avoided.

The readjustment of existing stocks and bonds presents difficulties which will be considered in very different ways by different classes of persons. The "granger" element, for instance, would cut off the holder of "watered stock" with a shilling. Fortunately, if we take time enough, we can arrange this matter with no shadow of injustice. To illustrate: The government can purchase the A. B. & C. road outright at its market value, which, owing to inflated prices and watered securities, is perhaps $3,000,000. It is desired to wipe out $1,000,000 of this to place the road upon its proper basis. The government issues 3 per cent. guaranteed ten-year bonds upon the road and leases it at an annual rental of 6 per cent. on what it has paid. At the time the bonds are due, the accumulation of rentals over interest is more than sufficient to pay off $1,000,000 of the bonds, while the remainder are renewed on the permanent basis.

The author is well aware that a very strong prejudice exists against the lending by the government of its credit to private corporations. This prejudice--which has perhaps already been sufficient to condemn the plan, as thus far presented, in the mind of the reader--he believes to be a very wise and well founded one. The assumption by the government of any risk in connection with corporate enterprise is highly undesirable. It is now to be noted that this objection is wholly overcome; for, notwithstanding the fact that the government guarantees the bonds of the railways, it is not proposed that it shall really assume any risk, as will be seen from the further description of the powers and obligations of the operating corporations.

These should be essentially private companies, but there should be two or three representatives of the government on the Board of Directors. They should be required to operate the roads in a safe, efficient, and economical manner, and to keep accurate and simple records, open to the inspection of the Government Commissioners, of the receipts and expenditures on every separate line of road. The rates of fare and freight should be, first of all, stable. When once fixed they should neither be raised nor lowered except by the direction of the Government Railway Commissioners. Next--and this is the cardinal feature of the whole plan--it should be the endeavor to fix the rates of fare and freight at such a point that the total receipts would be sufficient, first, to pay the whole expense of operating and maintaining the road; second, to pay the annual rental of 3?per cent. interest on the cost of the road; and, third, an annual dividend to the stockholders of the operating company of from 4 to 8 per cent. The capital stock of the operating company should be fixed by law at about 1?times the actual cost of rolling stock and machinery. The operating company should be allowed to issue only one class of securities, and these should represent at par the actual cash capital invested by the operating company.

Under this plan it is evident that every community would pay its equitable share of the cost of transportation, since the rates would be based on the cost of service.[6] Instead of roads running along, bankrupt for years, as now, we would have every community paying for its transportation facilities just what it cost to furnish them. But if, on any road, such a rule would raise the rates above a certain prescribed maximum point, then the rate could be lowered, if necessary, to a point where it was only great enough to pay the operating expenses; and part or all the bond interest would be paid out of the government railway fund.

[6] It should be explained that it is only proposed to base the rates as a whole upon the cost of service. As regards the relative rates on different commodities, the author, in common with all who have given careful study to the question, recognizes that the only equitable principle for proportioning rates is the much maligned one of "charging [in proportion to] what the traffic will bear." The argument against this principle is so very plausible that, until he had given the

subject thorough study he held a diametrically opposite opinion.

To make plain to the reader that this is really the only equitable principle, the following illustration may serve: A coal-mine operator and a sewing-machine manufacturer build together a railroad to carry their respective products to a market. They will fix the total rates of freight at such a point as to just pay the cost of service; but it is required to find what relative rates each should be equitably charged on the shipments from his works. Evidently, to have the rates perfectly equitable, they must be in exact proportion to the benefit which each party derives from the use of the road. But this benefit which each derives is measured by the profits which each makes from his business; and this profit, in turn, is the measure of the amount each can afford to pay for the use of the road,--that is to say, "what the traffic will bear." Q. E. D.

"But," the objector says, "is it not true that when you limit the profits of the companies and base rates on cost of service you take away all incentive to economy and careful operation? The public, and not the company, gain if the cost of service is reduced; so why should the manager exert himself to economize? This very same principle has been tried. Many States have chartered railway corporations, and provided that fares and freight rates should be reduced when dividends exceeded a certain per cent., or else that a percentage of the surplus earnings, above the amount necessary to earn, say 10 per cent. dividends, should be paid into the State treasury. Of course the railway corporations who have been able to earn surplus dividends which they were not permitted to pay, have been sharp enough to spend their surplus on their own property instead of turning it over to the State treasury. How is it possible, then, to base rates on cost of service and still leave the incentive to economy, frugality, and efficiency which exists, when the corporation is permitted to make all the profits it can?"

To discover a means of overcoming this difficulty, let us see how it is overcome under competition. A man invents a new machine, for instance, which effects a saving in the cost of some manufacturing process of 50 per cent. One manufacturer adopts it because it greatly increases his profits, and one by one his competitors follow suit. The competition between them cuts the prices lower and lower, till finally the consumers of the goods get all the benefit from the saving effected by the new machine, and the manufacturers' profits are no greater than they were originally. But the important point to be noted is this, that the benefit to the manufacturer continued long enough to repay him for introducing the machine. So in our attempts to base railway rates upon cost of service, we must permit the profit from the introduction of economies, the use of improved appliances, etc., to be gathered by the railway company long enough to induce it to work toward that end.

All we need to do to effect this end is to somewhat delay the change in rates to correspond to change in cost of service. As already stated, it is most necessary that rates should be stable, and it is proposed to make any change, either advance or reduction, only through the action of a Government Commission. Now, suppose that some such clause as this forms a part of our railway law: "upon the petition of any railway corporation, or of not less than twenty-five patrons of any single 'railway district,' it shall be the duty of the Railway Commission to investigate regarding a readjustment of rates to correspond more closely to the cost of service. If it shall be found that in the given 'railway district' the net receipts over the operating expenses and fixed charges have been for one year not less than 9 per cent. on the capital of the operating company invested in the given railway district; and that for two successive years they have been not less than 8 per cent.; or, if they have been for one year 8 per cent., and for two years 7 per cent., and it shall be proven to the satisfaction of the Commission, that any due and proper measure of economy, to which the attention of the officers was called in writing has been wilfully neglected, or that any uncalled for and manifestly extravagant expenditures have been entered into during that time, then it shall be the duty of the Commission to lower the rates. If it shall be found that for one year the net earnings have been less than 3?per cent., and for two years less than 4?per cent., unless it shall be proven that this deficit has been fostered by neglect of due economy, or by extravagant expenditure as aforesaid, the rates shall be raised. In all cases where rates are readjusted, it shall be the endeavor of the Commission to set them at such a point that the net earnings will equal 6 per cent. on the capital stock."

The provision requiring two years of excess or deficiency before a change, would be necessary to avoid the fluctuations which occur in single seasons. Every piece of economy is so much gain to the stockholders, and its benefit is received for at least two years. It must be remembered that in any railway corporation, as at present conducted, none but the highest of the managing officials have any personal interest in the profit from operations. It may well be believed, therefore, that the measure of economy and efficiency effected would be at least as great as now. As this plan also contemplates government representation on the Board of Directors, any action by the higher officials to evade the law would be unlikely to occur.

The receipts of a company operating say 30,000 miles of railway and carrying its traffic at fixed rates would vary but little from year to year; and its stock would be so largely held by investors and would vary so little in price that there would be very little speculation in it. To bankrupt the company would be an impossibility, since its receipts would always be regulated to preserve its revenue, although not so strictly but that the company would still have every incentive to cultivate traffic by offering good facilities, and to economize at the same time by the introduction of improved methods.

No doubt it can be shown where every detail of the foregoing plan leaves loop-holes for abuses to creep in. It will be much the same with any plan whatever. The questions to be asked are, would abuses, waste and stealing be any more likely to occur than under any other plan? Could they be any more prevalent than they are now,--bearable only because we are calloused to them? Of course, the foregoing is a mere outline of the general principles of the plan. Details which readily suggest themselves would, of course, be necessary to carry out the principle successfully.

That some attempt should be made in this connection to solve the perplexing problem of strikes on railway lines is proven by the memorable engineers' strike on the Chicago, Burlington, & Quincy system. Perhaps a provision requiring every employ?and officer to hold at least a certain number of shares in the operating company in proportion to his salary would help to solve the labor problem; and it might give the higher officers a greater interest in their work than they always show.

The author has deemed it worth while to outline the foregoing plan for the equitable control of railway monopolies with considerable fulness, because, to a very great extent, the principles followed in the design of this plan are applicable to a great number of other monopolies. These important principles are: (1) Government protection to the owners of fixed capital so that the public may obtain the use of it at the lowest possible rate of interest. (2) The operation of monopolies by corporations rather than by the government, thus securing the increased efficiency of private over official management. (3) Securing to the people at large the benefit of the monopoly by basing the prices for its product on cost of service. (4) But leaving a suitable incentive for the company's managers to maintain economy and efficiency in its operations. (5) Government representation in the directorate controlling the ordinary affairs of the company.

It is evident that the plan just outlined for railways would be especially well adapted, with but slight changes, for the control of the telegraph lines of the country.

* * * * *

We will next consider the monopolies discussed in Chapter III. It seems too plain to need proof that our mines and quarries are certain to have a steady increase in value as we use up the easily worked surface deposits and have to dig deeper shafts and develop the poorer deposits to supply the demand. In the case of any metals or minerals of which the deposits are so abundant, easily worked, and widely scattered, that the number of evenly matched competitors is great enough to ensure steady competition, the public will get the benefit of the especial gift of Nature, and its owner can receive little more than an ordinary return for his labor and capital. But, as we have already amply shown, in the production of a great number of minerals and metals competition has been killed, or is heavily handicapped by the vast advantages of a few bonanza mines, and the public is being taxed millions of dollars for that which belongs to it by right.

How long is this condition to continue? Must all succeeding generations pay for coal, copper, zinc, lead, nickel, marble, oil, gas, and various other products of our mother-earth just what those who control the chief deposits choose to ask? Because a pioneer stumbles upon a valuable mine, shall the sole right to use the product of that mine be secured "to him, his heirs and assigns" forever?

Suppose, now, that each of the several States were to acquire the title to all the productive mines, quarries, and mineral wealth within its borders, and enact laws providing that future discoverers of minerals on land where they are not now known to exist should be liberally rewarded, if the discovery proved valuable, but the minerals should belong to the State and not to the owner of the land. The same principle which we found to apply in the case of the railways would serve here in readjusting values, viz.: the difference in the rates of interest on safe investments and on risky ones. When acquired, the mines should be leased to private parties for operation. In the case of coal-mines and perhaps of iron, it would be well to copy largely from the scheme proposed for railway operation, viz.: place all the business in the hands of a single company, which should thus be enabled to carry on its business on the largest possible scale; do away with wasteful competition, and aim to regulate prices to provide a certain reasonable steady income on its capital to the mining company.

For mines of copper, zinc, lead, and similar metals, it would be best to pursue a different plan, and simply provide by statute that such mines should be leased for short terms of years to the bidder who would offer to sell his product at the lowest price per ton at the mines, all lettings and relettings to be publicly advertised, and the successful bidder to give bonds for the faithful performance of his contract. It is difficult to see how, under these conditions, a combination to defeat competition could be formed. Relettings of expired leases would be frequent; and bidding by the selling price, a single competitor would be sufficient to break any combination. Of course the lease should specify a minimum product which the mine should furnish.

It would be advisable, too, that a manifest duty of the government, which should be undertaken even under present conditions, should be observed. It should be required to work the mine with due attention to saving the greatest possible amount of ore or mineral contained in the seam or vein.

The third class of monopolies, whose legal subjection to public control is acknowledged, are those connected with our municipal public works. There is already a widespread movement toward taking the control and operation of these out of the hands of private corporations, and placing it directly with the city government, and progress in this direction is very rapid. The author believes, however, that the general law already stated is applicable here. If the public works of States and of the nation are more economically and efficiently managed when in the hands of private parties, it is surely unwise, as a general rule, to entrust the operation of municipal works to the average city official. While it is in the highest degree desirable that water-works, gas, and electric-lighting plants, street railways, and the other municipal enterprises, discussed in Chapter V., should be owned by the municipality, their operation, in cases where the employment of considerable labor and the carrying on of intricate business and mechanical operations is involved, should in general be entrusted to private companies. In every case where the financial condition of the municipality obliges it to rely at first upon private corporations for the construction and ownership of its public works, the franchise should expire at the end of a short term of years, and the city should then have the privilege of purchasing the works at their actual cost.

As regards works for water supply, there can be little doubt that almost invariably the municipality should operate as well as own the works, for the administration of the works requires but a small amount of labor, and that of such a class that the city can safely carry it on. But gas or electric-light plants, both for street and resident lighting, should be operated by private companies.

These industries are making such rapid progress in the way of new processes, effecting both economy and improvement, that it is somewhat difficult to say what steps should be taken. Many are of the opinion that gas is destined to be entirely replaced by the electric light; but while this may eventually prove true, it will probably be a very long time before the existing gas-works cease to supply consumers. Thus the true solution of the problem seems to be that when a growing town nowadays wishes to establish a new lighting plant of its own, it should adopt electricity. But in the case of a town having gas-works already established, the municipality is safe in assuming their ownership.

As regards the operation of lighting plants in small towns, it would doubtless be best to lease the plant for short terms of years to the highest bidder, making sure that the call for proposals is widely circulated. Great cities, however, would find this policy unsatisfactory. If a ten-year lease of the Philadelphia gas-works, for instance, were advertised for sale to the highest bidder, there would be but few really close bidders upon it, and the danger of "a combination to defeat competition" would be great. It is at least worth considering whether such a plan as we proposed for railways could not be made feasible here. Let a corporation be chartered to operate the lighting plant of the city, and let the charter of the corporation provide that its rates shall be such as to pay an annual dividend upon its capital stock (fixed by law and not changeable) equal to the legal rate of interest in the State. Provided, that in no case should the rates be lowered unless the net profits in one year were more than 2 per cent. in excess of this rate, and that the excess for two consecutive years was more than 1?per cent. in excess of this rate. Provided also, that in no case should the rates be raised unless the deficit exceeded 1?per cent. in any year, and 1 per cent. for two consecutive years, and that it should be proven by the company that it had exercised all reasonable diligence, care, and economy in the management and operation of its business.

A certain proportion of the stock--less than a majority--should be held by the city; and the mayor should appoint directors to represent the city, at least one of whom should be personally conversant with the industry carried on by the company.

Although not often so considered, the matter of passenger transportation is a much more important matter in our greatest cities than either lighting or water supply. The laboring man, who has to pay perhaps twelve cents for the necessary ride back and forth to his work every day, feels this tax most severely. Suppose that under such an arrangement for street railways as we have outlined for gas and electric lighting companies the fare would be reduced to three cents. His savings from this source would amount to at least $18 per year. Counting the extra rides and those which his wife and children have to take, the annual saving would probably reach $25, a sum which to the average laboring man with a family dependent upon him means a great deal.

Our municipal monopolies are now taxing us that they may pay swollen dividends on millions of dollars of fictitious capital. It is quite time that the public recovered possession of the valuable franchises which are its rightful property, and managed them for its own benefit. The legal difficulties in regaining the title to these franchises are certainly not insuperable, and the readjustment of capitalization can be made on the principle outlined in the case of steam railways. To illustrate: The city of "Polis" purchases the works which supply it with water from the private company owning them, paying the average market value of the stock and bonds during five years past, which amounts, perhaps, to one and one half times the cost of the works. The revenue from the works has been sufficient, probably, to pay 8 per cent. on these securities. The city issues 3 per cent. ten-year bonds to raise funds for the purchase, and it then operates the works so as to gain a yearly revenue of 6 per cent., or 2 per cent. less than that gained by the private company. At the end of ten years the surplus income from the works is enough to pay more than one third the bonded indebtedness; and, if desired, the rest may be reissued as new bonds to run for a long period.

The three classes of monopolies just discussed--railways, mineral wealth, and municipal works--include practically all the monopolies which are generally acknowledged to be subject to the public control by virtue of their use of natural agents or the exercise of franchises granted by the public.

We will next consider the monopolies in trade, in manufacturing, and in the purchase and sale of labor, to see what steps should be taken to protect them from encroaching on the rights of the people. In exercising the right of the people at large to take control of these purely private industries from the hands of their owners, we are assuming a power which, like a strong medicine, may be as potent for evil as for good. Only extreme necessity should sanction its use, and its abuse must be carefully guarded against. It is not saying too much to assert that the abuse of this power has already become an evil. We have become so used to legislation for the benefit of special industries, that legislation for their injury does not seem to be regarded as the exercise of a dangerous prerogative. Thus we are threatened with a flood of laws to fix the prices in various industries now subject to monopoly, or to crush them out altogether by enacting some restrictive measure,--legislation which, by its directness, is apt to strike the average lawmaker very favorably, but which, it needs little wisdom to see, is the sure forerunner of abuses. The author trusts that nothing in this book may be construed as advocating or defending some of the crude and ill-considered attempts at anti-monopoly legislation already made, or that may be made in the future.

We have proven in the preceding chapters that, from the character of modern concentrated industry, a very large number of our manufactures must either exist as monopolies or else must engage in intense and wasteful competition. If the monopoly can be so managed that it shall carry on the industry economically, adopt improvements, keep up the character of its product, and keep the prices therefor so low as to make no more than ordinary profits, it would be for the public advantage that monopolies rather than competition should exist. Can we regulate monopolies to secure such results? If so, our problem will be solved.

The author has proposed for the first class of monopolies--those obtaining the benefit of natural agents and public franchises--government ownership of fixed capital and regulation of prices, with private operation and general management. But he is far from believing that such a plan would now be wise for regulating trusts. It may indeed be that, at some time in the future, many of the great staple manufactures will be formally established by the government as monopolies, and controlled in a similar way to that which we have outlined for the railway system; but it is so far in the future that we need not consider it in detail now. Under our present political organization it would be practically impossible for the government to undertake to regulate justly and equitably such an industry, for instance, as the steel-rail manufacture. We have set our State, national, and municipal governments a hard enough task in the preceding pages of this chapter, in bringing under public control our monopolies of transportation and communication and our productive mines; and although it is a work possible of accomplishment, it will need good statesmanship to carry it out. By the time that task is accomplished, a similar plan, improved as experience will then suggest, may perhaps be found available for the regulation of the important manufacturing industries.

We decide, then, that it is for the public advantage at present that both the ownership and operation of manufacturing industries and of trade must remain in private hands. The next question is, will the greatest advantage to the public be secured by starting a crusade to re-establish competition and break up all existing monopolies in manufacturing and trade; or by taking the opposite course, legalizing monopolies and so regulating them by law that they shall be prevented from making undue profits by laying an exorbitant tax upon the public?

Practically all the efforts made or proposed thus far for remedying the evils of monopolies in manufacturing and trade have had for their purpose the re-establishment of competition. The investigation to which the first part of this book was devoted shows the wide extent of the movement to restrict competition. Is it possible to wholly counteract this? All our study of the laws of competition seems to show that the tendency of modern competition is to destroy itself by its own intensity. Certainly all the strenuous efforts to keep it alive by the force of legal enactment and public opinion have thus far proved unavailing. There are now, probably, at least a million persons in the United States who are directly or indirectly interested in unlawful contracts in restraint of competition; and among them are included many of the best financiers and most enterprising business men of the country. Certainly those who propose to drive these men into a renewal of competitive strife contrary to their will have set themselves a very difficult task.

Let us consider the opposite alternative. It cannot be a good thing to have such a great proportion of the active business men of the country, who bear the highest personal character, engaged in illegal contracts. Let us therefore take them within the pale of the law. They seem to be determined to make contracts with each other in restraint of competition; and believe, indeed, that they are forced to do it by modern conditions of trade. Suppose we were to legalize these contracts and permit the establishment of monopolies. What can we then do to protect the public from extortion in prices and adulteration in its products on the part of the monopoly?

In the first place, now that we have legalized monopolies there is no more excuse for secrecy. To work in darkness and privacy befits law-breakers, but is needless for legitimate enterprises. Let the law provide that every contract for the restriction of competition shall be in writing, and that a copy shall be filed, as a deed for real estate is filed now, with the proper city or town officer where the property affected is situate, and also with the Secretary of State where the contract is made. Certainly no honest man will object to this provision. The contention has been made that contracts to restrict competition were necessarily kept secret because they were "without the pale of the law." Very well; we have legalized them. There can be no further defense of secrecy. If any now refuse to make public their contracts to restrict competition, the refusal is evidence that the contract is for the injury of the public or some competitor and therefore properly punishable. We shall now know just what monopolies exist; just what is their strength, and for just how long a time their members are bound. Let us next see what measures we can adopt to prevent these legalized monopolies from practising extortion upon the public and abusing the power they have gained by the combination.

The first important means to secure this which the author would suggest is simply an extension of the common-law principle of non-discrimination. A man in conducting certain sorts of business is permitted to do as he chooses. He may sell to one person and refuse to sell to another; he may give to one and withhold from another. But if he enters business as the keeper of an inn or as a common carrier of passengers or freight, he can no longer exercise partiality.

He has elected to become a necessary servant of the public, and as such he is bound to serve impartially all who apply. In the same way a manufacturer while he engages in business under the usual laws of competition, may sell to whom he pleases and exercise such preference as he chooses. But when he combines with all other manufacturers of the same sort in a combination to restrict competition, he and his allies voluntarily change their relation to the public. Is it not true that they do actually elect to become necessary servants of the public--far more necessary, indeed, than the inn-keeper or the stage-coach driver,--and ought they not therefore to be placed under similar legal restrictions?

In every case where combination or consolidation restricts competition in an industry, one effect produced is an increase in the power over the public which the industry possesses. But this increased power over the public, thus voluntarily assumed, must inevitably carry with it increased responsibility to the public. It is the duty of the government to see that this responsibility is legally enforced.

This first principle, then, should be embodied in a law providing, in substance, that every person or firm entering into a contract to restrict competition should, so long as that contract was in force, be debarred from showing any preference in his or its purchases and sales, by giving more or less favorable prices to any person or firm than those quoted to any other person or firm. To enforce this requirement and prevent its evasion it is necessary to provide also that prices shall be public and that they shall not be altered without due notice. The requirement of publicity might be best effected by providing that the contract restricting competition should contain a schedule of prices, which would usually be the case in any event.

While this may seem like quite an assumption of authority on the part of the State, it is exactly what trusts and trade associations are striving to effect, though with the important qualification that when occasion, in the shape of an obnoxious competitor, requires, they wish to be at liberty to put prices up or down at short notice and exercise their preferences as they choose.

Let us now see what we would effect by the enforcement of this principle of non-discrimination. We have explained in the chapter on combinations in trade how one monopoly gains strength by alliance with another; as when the firms belonging to the car-spring combination made a contract with the steel combination by which that monopoly agreed to sell to them at a reduced price and to make an extra rate to their competitors. Under this law it would be impossible to found one monopoly upon the favors of another in this manner.

The obnoxious trade boycott, too, which is now becoming so common, would be effectually checked. And the scheme for crushing out a rival by giving all his customers specially favorable rates would no longer be practicable. The fact is that if we can stop the discriminations which the monopolies have practised, we shall cure a large share of the evils they have caused. It may be said that the courts will already punish many conspiracies of this sort; but a monopoly which is already breaking the law by its contracts of combination, finds in its methods of doing business plenty of chances to evade the laws against conspiracy. Certainly with a properly drawn law with reference to the publicity and stability of prices, it should be possible to practically wipe out the evil of discrimination by monopolies. It is also to be noted that the requirement of non-discrimination and of public and stable prices would bring profit in doing away with the waste of competition.

We have now to inquire what means it is possible to take to ensure that the prices charged by the monopoly shall not only be the same to all, but that they shall not in themselves be so exorbitant that the monopoly will reap large profits at the public expense. How can we keep the prices charged by the monopoly from rising far above the point where they would stand if free competition were in force? Two methods are open to us. We may keep down the monopoly's rates by what we will call potential competition, or we may reduce them directly by legislative enactment.

The right of the public to take this latter course may be defended on the ground that the monopoly has voluntarily made itself a necessary public servant, and in that capacity offers to the public its goods. While it is true that the people permit the monopoly to become a necessary public servant and protect it in the contracts by which it restricts competition, it is also true that the monopoly cannot justly make merchandise of the necessities of the people. The public may allow a combination to obtain control of all the sugar refineries, for instance, and protect the combination in its formation. But suppose the owners of the combination then say: "The people are obliged to have sugar and we control the supply. We will set a high price on sugar, therefore, because we know that they will pay it rather than go without." They are then making the necessity of the public a source of gain, and it cannot be believed that this will be permanently suffered.

The serious difficulty in fixing by direct government action the prices which a monopoly of this sort shall charge, is that we cannot stop at that point. When once the government steps in to do so radical a thing as to fix the price which a monopoly shall charge, it becomes in equity responsible to the owners of that monopoly for the maintenance of their incomes from their capital invested. If their profits have been so reduced by this action as to seriously injure the value of their property, they have a legal right to claim compensation from the state for the injury it has done them. And in almost every case they would set up the claim that their property had been thus injured. To determine the point at which reasonable prices and reasonable profits become extortionate prices and unjust profits is a task requiring expert knowledge and the most comprehensive judgment, aided by the most accurate statistics. To impose this task on our already overburdened courts would permanently block the wheels of justice, and would give to the judicial department of government a work which its machinery is wholly unsuited to carry on.

It seems evident, therefore, that when it becomes necessary for the state to directly fix prices to be charged by monopolies, a more radical step should be taken. The monopoly should be established on a permanent basis, and the state should have some part in its direct control.

Discarding, therefore, direct action by the state to fix prices as inexpedient, for the present, at least, let us see what we can effect by means of "potential" competition, which term we will use to signify that competition which may be established in any monopolized industry if the inducements offered are sufficiently great. It must be remembered that nowadays men of capital and enterprise are always on the look-out for every opportunity to invest money and expend their industry where it will bring the greatest returns. If any monopoly seems to be making large returns, people are generally ready to believe that it is making twice as great profits as it really is; and some one is quite likely to start in as a competitor, if there is a prospect of large profits. Now we wish to do two things. We wish to make it so easy for new competitors to enter the field against a monopoly that its managers will keep their profits down in order not to call in any new competitors. We also wish to so modify the intensity of competition between the monopoly and the new competitor that the latter may have a chance at least of being repaid for its expenditure in entering the field. The simplest and best of the legal provisions which we may enforce to this end is the one already stated of non-discrimination. The monopoly can no longer reduce its price to apply to only the limited field in which the new competitor works, but must reduce its prices everywhere to meet those made by the rival. In the case of monopolies in trade and all monopolies in manufacturing in which the fixed capital required is but small, this is all that would be needed to encourage the establishment of new competitors and discourage the monopoly from grasping after undue profits from the public.

In the case of those manufacturing monopolies in which a large fixed capital must be invested at the start by any new competitor, we have a much more difficult problem. It is true that in this case the monopoly itself has more at stake; and this may induce the starting up of new competitors simply to be bought out by the trust,--a sort of blackmailing operation which is certainly repugnant in its character. It might be possible to provide that rates charged by the monopoly must be so stable that a competitor would have a chance to establish itself before the monopoly could bring its own rates down. It might be possible to force the monopoly to keep all its factories in operation, and thus oblige it to keep down its price in order to dispose of its products; but there are evident practical difficulties in the way of enforcing such laws. It seems a great pity that just now, when to find some employment of prison convicts in some manner that will not "compete with free labor," and thus displease the labor interests, seems an impossibility, we cannot set the convicts at work to compete with the trusts and bring down their profits to a reasonable point. Surely the labor party would find no fault with this use of convict competition.

There is one step, however, which we can take, and whose effect would certainly be very great; in its desirability, apart from questions of monopoly, all honest men are practically united. We can reform our laws regarding corporate management. It is a mild arraignment compared to what is deserved, to say that our present laws regarding the formation and management of corporations, taking the country as a whole, are a shame to the people and a disgrace to the men who made them. They seem designed to place a premium on fraud and knavery, and to assist the professional projector and stock manipulator in reaping gains from innocent--generally very innocent--stockholders. Now a real reform in our corporation laws would greatly simplify our work in controlling monopolies. Let us have no more stock-watering of any sort at any time in a corporation's life. Let us have no more "income bonds" which yield no income, and "preferred stock" in which another is preferred after all. Two classes of securities are enough for an honest corporation, and the public interest requires the charter of no other class of companies. Let us have done, too, with the iniquitous custom of one corporation holding another's stock or bonds. With a few such simple reforms as these effected, the holders of stock in our corporations would have some idea where they stand and what their securities represent, and would take some interest in the control of their property.

With these reforms, in the case of every corporation making a contract to restrict competition, it would be required that the company make public annually a full statement of its receipts, expenditures, and profits. Every monopoly would stand before the public then in its true position, and every one would know if it were making 50 per cent. per annum on the actual capital invested, or only 5 per cent. With these facts made public, if any monopoly ventured to raise its price till it reaped unusual profits, some of the heaviest consumers of the monopolized product would be very apt to start a factory of their own in opposition. It is to be remembered that under the law of non-discrimination the monopolies would be prevented from currying favor with the large consumers by giving them specially favorable prices. It is now common to do this, as it removes the danger of combination among these important customers to compete with the monopoly.

To sum up, the chief features of the plan proposed for the control of monopolies in manufacture and trade are as follows: Make contracts to restrict competition, legal and binding, instead of illegal and void as now. But; provide that every such contract shall be filed for public inspection; that prices charged by the combination shall be public, stable, and absolutely unvarying to all; that the affairs of the combination shall be managed according to a consistent and stringent corporation law; and that an annual report of the operations of the combination be made to a public commission.

Contrast this with the existing law upon this important subject. In Judge Barrett's decision in the Sugar Trust case he said:

"The development of judicial thought, in regard to contracts in restraint of trade, has been especially marked. The ancient doctrine upon that head has been weakened and modified to such a degree that but little if any of it is left. Indeed, excessive competition may sometimes result in actual injury to the public; and anti-competitive contracts, to avert personal ruin, may be perfectly reasonable. It is only when such contracts are publicly oppressive that they become unreasonable, and are condemned as against public policy."

This is probably the best statement of the present status of the common law upon this subject now extant. But what a path to endless litigation does it open! Who shall draw the line where a contract to restrain competition ceases to be beneficial and lawful, and becomes an injury to the public welfare? Must this be left to judge and jury? If so, the responsibilities of our already overburdened Courts are vastly increased.

In contrast with such a policy as this, the plan before presented certainly promises definiteness in the place of uncertainty; and treats all contracts in restraint of competition with impartiality. It is believed that the effect of its enforcement would be a great reduction in the tax now levied on us by monopolies.

There is yet one way, however, in which all these monopolies that we have found it so difficult to devise a plan to deal with--the manufacturers' trusts-- may be quickly and certainly reduced. Our heavy tariff on imported goods, by protecting manufacturers from foreign competition, and thus reducing the number of possible competitors, has undeniably been a chief reason why trusts have appeared and grown wealthy in this country before any other. The author has purposely refrained, as far as possible, from reference to the relation of the tariff to monopolies; for the question has been so hotly fought over, and the real facts concerning it have been so garbled and distorted, that people are not yet ready to consider it in an unprejudiced way. This much, however, no one can gainsay. We hold in our hands the means to at any time reduce the prices and profits of practically all our monopolies in manufacturing to a reasonable basis, by simply cutting down the duty on the products of foreign manufactories. Now, if after our plan just described is in force, the managers of any monopoly choose to be so reckless as to raise its prices to a point where its published reports will show it to be making enormous profits, thus tempting new competitors to enter the field and breeding public hostility, all honest protectionists and free-traders will be quite apt to unite in a demand that the "protection" under which this monopoly is permitted to tax the public be taken away.

If only we could find in any possible plan so excellent a solution of the problem of labor monopolies as a reduction of the tariff offers us in the case of trusts! The question is so complex a one that it is hardly possible to consider it here, except very briefly. Certainly, if we legalize combinations to restrict competition among capitalists, we should among laborers as well. Indeed, the decay of the old common-law principle, that such contracts were against public policy, and that such combinations were punishable, has been more marked in the case of trade unions than anywhere else. Besides this, as long as employers have the right to kill competition in the purchase of labor, workmen should certainly have the right to avoid competition in its sale. But to prevent by force other competitors from taking the field, if they choose, against any labor combination, is an infringement of the personal liberty guaranteed to every man by the Constitution, and can by no means be lawfully permitted.

If workingmen only understood how much the apparent gain when they win in a strike is overbalanced by their loss in the higher prices which they have to pay for the necessaries of life, and in the reduced demand for labor, they would be as anxious to protect capital as they now are--some of them--to injure it. The strikes make timid the men who have capital to invest. They will not loan their money to business men, builders, manufacturers, or any one who wishes to use it to employ workmen, except at a higher rate of interest, to pay for the increased risk. Hence, the cost of the capital used in production is greater, and the price the public has to pay for the product must be greater.

Again, when men have to pay higher rates of interest for the money they borrow they are slower to engage in new enterprises. Mr. A. a builder, intended to put up a block of a dozen houses this season, which would have tended to reduce rents; but the fear of strikes, with their attendant damage and loss, has prevented him from borrowing money at less than 8 per cent. interest. He concludes that, on the whole, this will eat up so much of his profits that he will not build. Is it not too plain to need proof that the moral influence alone of the strikes has robbed the workmen at every point? And this is one of a thousand cases in a hundred different industries.

The plans we have discussed for the treatment of monopolies have for their object a benefit to the people at large, by enabling them to purchase the products of industry and of natural wealth free from the tax now levied upon them by monopolies. If we can effect this, we shall not have a millennium; there will still be injustice and suffering enough in the world; but we shall have reduced the pressure upon the men who work with their hands for their daily bread, enough so that we shall no longer see the strange spectacle of over-production and hunger and nakedness existing side by side. Men's desires were made by an All-wise Creator to be always in advance of their ability to gratify them. And the commercial supply of that ability--the supply of men willing to work--ought always to be behind the demand for men.

It seems beyond dispute, then, that whatever will remove these obstructions to the wheels of production will increase the demand for labor, as well as increase the wages of labor by lowering the prices of the necessaries of life. This the plan we have discussed promises to do, and it also promises to benefit the whole people by lowering the cost of monopolized articles.

The men and women who work with their hands, and those dependent on them, form 97 per cent. of the population of the country. Instead of combining to stop production in this shop or that factory, why not join hands to work for reforms in the interest of the whole people? Be sure that in so doing, organized labor will have the hearty co-operation, and leadership if need be, of the best men in every class of society.

But while the reforms proposed promise great and important benefits to the workers on whom the tax laid by monopoly falls most cruelly, the question, "What shall fix the rate of wages, if competition cannot?" is still left undecided. The best answer the author can make to this is as follows: The monopoly formed by the trade unions in the sale of labor is unnatural, because the number of competing units is great instead of small. As new competitors must continually arise, the monopoly can never be successful without the use of unlawful means. If it raises the price of labor above what free competition would determine, it as truly lays a tax on the whole people as did the copper monopoly. On the other hand, we must recognize the fact that competition is now often absent in the purchase of labor, and this is a chief and sufficient cause for the existing attempts to kill competition in its sale. But this is largely due to the fact that the supply of labor is now in excess of the demand. When instead of signs everywhere, "No one need apply for employment here," we see placards, "Men wanted; high prices to good workmen," then competition will assert itself in the purchase of labor.

In regard to the first class of industries, those utilizing natural agents, which we proposed to place under the care of the state, it is evident that we can permit no strikes there. Our transportation lines, our mines, our gas-works, our water supplies, are to be operated for the benefit of the whole people, and no labor monopoly can be permitted to stop them. The plan that might be adopted to prevent interruptions in these industries has been already referred to. The author would suggest a similar plan for the benefit of labor in general. Suppose that in the charter of a manufacturing corporation, a certain portion of the stock in small-sized shares was set aside for the employees required to operate the mill. Let each employé be required to hold a certain number of shares in proportion to his wages; to purchase them when he begins to work, and to return them when he leaves the service of the corporation; the price in all cases to be par. In case he leaves without giving a certain notice, he should forfeit a certain proportion of his stock. If, on the other hand, he is discharged without an equal notice, he should receive the full amount of his stock, and a sum in addition equal to the penalty which he would have incurred had he broken the contract. Who will deny that such a move would be vastly to the interest of both parties, the employer and employed. Is not a protection needed by the workman against the power of the employer to turn him adrift at any time without a penny?

Finally it must be said that the labor question, more than any other connected with monopoly, needs solution through the influence of the principles of Christian fraternity. In the last analysis, every man sells to his brother men his service and receives his food, clothing, and shelter in return. We may execute justice never so well, and regulate never so nicely the wages of men by the law of supply and demand, there will still be special cases demanding and deserving to be treated by the rules of brotherly charity. The strong were given their power that they might aid the feeble; and they who fall behind in the struggle for position are not to be blotted out by the brute law of the survival of the fittest, but cared for as the noblest instincts of humanity prompt.

* * * * *

I am well aware that the indictment which conservative critics will be apt to bring against the plans for the equitable control of monopolies presented in this chapter is that they are too novel, and that they require too much of an upheaval of existing institutions for their accomplishment. The conservative man is invariably in favor of getting along with things as they are. The answer to be made to this is, that no candid man who will make a thorough study of the present status of monopoly and of the attempts to control it can be conservative. The present status of monopolies is just neither to their owners nor to the public. They are plundering the public as much or as little as they choose; and the sovereign people are submitting to it and taking their revenge by passing retaliatory laws intended to ruin the monopolies if possible. These legislative "strikes" are thus especially well calculated to foster extortion on the part of the owners of monopolies, who naturally wish to make what profits they can before some piece of legislation is put through to destroy the industry they have built up.

In contrast to this are the plans proposed in this chapter. They offer to establish a definite relation between the public and the monopolies, and a permanent and stable foundation for each industry they affect in place of the present fickle and ever changing one.

There is another class of critics who may complain that the plan proposed leaves too much power still in the hands of the monopolists, and gives the government too small a part in their management. The answer to this is very evident. We have found the cardinal value of the system of individual competition to be that it tends by a process of natural selection to bring the men of greatest ability into the control and management of our industries; while the vital weakness in the management of industry by government is the fact that the sovereign people does not choose the wisest and most honest men to control its affairs. Men may well say that if they are to be robbed it had better be by a corporation, where innocent stockholders will receive part of the benefit, than by dishonest officials of government.

The ultimate remedy for the evils of monopoly, therefore, lies with the people. When they will choose to control their affairs the men of greatest wisdom and honor; when each man will exercise the same care in choosing men to care for the public business that he does in caring for his own private interests, then we can safely trust far greater responsibilities to our government than is now prudent.

There is no more important lesson to impress on the minds of the toiling millions who are growing restless under the burdens of monopoly than this: The only remedy for monopoly is control; the only power that can control is government; and to have a government fit to assume these momentous duties, all good men and true must join hands to put only men of wisdom and honor in places of public trust.

There is a virtue which shone in all brightness when this nation was born, not alone in the hearts of the commander-in-chief and his brother heroes, but in the hearts of the men and women who gave themselves to their country's service. It glowed with all fervor when, a quarter of a century ago, the North fought to sustain what the fathers had created, and the rank and file of the South gave their lives and all they had for what they deemed a righteous and noble cause. Though the robust spirit of partisanship may seem for a time to have crowded out from men's hearts the love of their country, surely that love still remains; and in the days of new import which dawn upon us, in the virtue of PATRIOTISM will be found a sufficient antidote for the vice of monopoly.

###